Reformation in Responsibility

A New Ethic for a New Era

Addressed to the
People
of the
United States of America

Rit Varriale

Printed in
North Carolina
First Printing, MMXII

Reformation in Responsibility

© 2012 by Rit Varriale

Published by DVPUBLISHERS

All rights reserved. No part of this book may be reproduced or transmitted without written permission of the publisher. For information regarding permission to reprint material from this book, please e-mail your request to *admin@RinR.org*.

Scripture quotations marked (NKJV) are taken from the New King James Version®. Copyright © 1982 by Thomas Nelson, Inc. Used by permission. All rights reserved.

Scripture quotations marked (NRSV) are from New Revised Standard Version Bible, copyright © 1989 National Council of the Churches of Christ in the United States of America. Used by permission. All rights reserved.

Quotations designated (NIV) are from THE HOLY BIBLE: NEW INTERNATIONAL VERSION®. NIV®. Copyright © 1973, 1978, 1984 by International Bible Society. Used by permission of Zondervan Publishing House. All rights reserved

Scripture quotations marked (NLT) are from the Holy Bible, New Living Translation. Copyright © 1996. Used by permission of Tyndale House Publishers.

Scripture quotations marked (NAS) are taken from the NEW AMERICAN STANDARD BIBLE, © Copyright The Lockman Foundation 1960, 1962, 1963, 1968, 1971, 1972, 1973, 1975, 1977, 1988, 1995. Used by permission.

Library of Congress Control Number: 2012933037
Reformation in responsibility: a new ethic for a new era / Rit Varriale

ISBN 978-0-9851545-0-9
1. Religion and philosophy / social responsibility / church and state / theology / ethics

Cover logo by KrisGissDesigns

Printed in North Carolina, United States of America

Quote from The First Epistle of Clement is from Ante-Nicene Fathers. Vol. 1. The Apostolic Fathers, Justin Martyr, Irenaeus. The First Epistle of Clement to the Corinthians. Hendrickson Publishers, 2004. Pages 5-6. Used by permission.

DVPublishers is a Division of
The Appian Company, LLC.
info@theappian.com

Contents

Introduction v

Chapter One: The Perfect Philosophical Storm 9
Essay 1: The Rise of Individualism 11
Essay 2: The Query of Evolution 16
Essay 3: The Modern Scientific Error 21
Essay 4: Life, Liberty, & the Pursuit of Unhappiness 26
Essay 5: Adolescent America... 32

Chapter Two: The Separation Of Thought And State.... 37
Essay 6: A Government of the Courts for the Minority... 39
Essay 7: Taxation & Economic Tyranny 44
Essay 8: Social Security & the Sanctity of Marriage 50
Essay 9: Welfare Education 55
Essay 10: State of Confusion... 60

Chapter 3: Theological Individualism 67
Essay 11: The Protestant Reformation & Pandora's Box . 70
Essay 12: Individualism & American Revivalism 75
Essay 13: Welfare Theology & the Problem of Hell........ 81
Essay 14: Failing to Succeed.. 86
Essay 15: Agnostic Preachers & Empty Pews 91

Chapter Four: The Church In The 21st Century 97
Essay 16: Responsible Theology 101
Essay 17: A New Ethic for a New Era............................ 105
Essay 18: Majority Rights & Privatized Religion 110
Essay 19: Civil Disobedience... 115
Essay 20: The Reformation 121

This book is dedicated to the people of the United States for the glory of God. Change will only occur when it occurs within you.

> Every kind of honor and happiness was bestowed upon you, and then was fulfilled that which is written, "My beloved did eat and drink, and was enlarged and became fat, and kicked." Hence, flowed emulation and envy, strife and sedition, persecution and disorder, war and captivity. So the worthless rose up against the honored, those of no reputation against such as were renowned, the foolish against the wise, the young against those advanced in years. For this reason, righteousness and peace are now departed from you, inasmuch as everyone abandons the fear of God and has become blind…

The First Epistle of Clement to the Corinthians c. 100 C.E.

INTRODUCTION

This is not a book that I wanted to write, insomuch as, many of the social issues addressed in these essays (e.g. taxation, same-sex marriage, labor laws, etc.) are issues that I prefer to leave to others for debate. However, given our current social climate, I was burdened to write this book. It is impossible to ignore the issues presented in this work, and there is no doubt that our handling of these issues will determine the future success or failure of our nation. Every nation has its struggles. Every generation has its crises, and this generation of Americans is no exception. Our current struggle is more difficult than any military conflict on foreign soil—it is a philosophical and theological struggle within our own borders. The crisis of our generation is a crisis of responsibility. Our finances, our morals, our judicial decisions, our educational system, our welfare programs, etc. are all upside down because we have failed to address adequately the issue of individual responsibility. For the last few centuries, Western philosophy and theology have been dominated by, what this work refers to as, irresponsible individualism. Instead of emphasizing the stability of our society, we have emphasized the individual's pursuit of happiness as the ultimate goal of society.

Undoubtedly, happiness is an essential part of life and it should be pursued, but not at the expense of fulfilling our responsibilities to God and to our society. Countless people have demonstrated that ignoring one's responsibilities and pursuing happiness at all costs ends in failure and disappointment. We, the people of the United States, have done this as a nation. We have taken the positive concept of individualism to such an extreme that we have created a culture marked by irresponsible individualism, that is, we are quick to make God and society responsible for the happiness of the individual, but we are reluctant to make the individual responsible to God and society. This is the reason we are frustrated and failing as a nation. Part of our problem is that we arrogantly reject common sense and traditional values, but solving our crisis is not as simple as going back to what we were at any given time in our past. It makes little sense to try and return to what we were. What we were got us where we are. Indeed, it was only a matter of time before our irresponsible emphasis on individual rights and happiness would manifest itself through social and political dysfunction. That time has come.

Morally, we can't differentiate between supporting equal rights and supporting immoral and socially unproductive lifestyles. Politically, most of our leaders are unable to look beyond their own personal gain and put the needs of the nation first. Economically, we are a nation of debt because individuals, families, and corporations believe the pursuit of happiness entitles them to live far beyond their financial means. Educationally, our public school system has evolved into a bureaucratic public daycare/sports program with standardized testing thrown in to justify our pedagogical façade. Judicially, our civil religion (a.k.a. Christianity) is, in the name of individual rights, suppressed by the courts. Environmentally, we have destroyed more of our planet in the last century than all the previous centuries put together. In short, we believe our individual needs are more important than family, society, the environment, and even more important than God. Now we are reaping what we have sown, and we are less happy for it.

We need a new direction. To find that new direction, we have to be humble enough to admit that we have failed to fulfill our responsibilities to our families, our society, our environment, and our God. Thus, the only thing that will change our nation is the willingness of our people to assume those responsibilities once again. Change will not come through a particular political party or religious denomination. Change will not come through the empty words of political leaders and presidents. It will not come through the voting procedures of a new Congress. Change will only come through the actions of the people. We, the people of the United States, need to change. The only question is: "Are we willing to change?" We have become so irresponsible and self-absorbed that the changes necessary to turn our nation around will not come easily. Yet, as hard as those changes may be, they are easier than the hardships that will follow if we refuse to change. Change is what this book is all about.

This book can easily be read in the course of an afternoon. However, that is not the intent of this work. This book is designed to foster reflection and discussion both of which are essential for change. This book does not boast of any new concepts. If anything, this work is taking a discussion that has already been going on and it is rearranging the conversation points in order to gain a better understanding of our national crisis. For this reason, the tone of this work is conversational not academic. Hence, there are no footnotes or bibliographies. For the next month, consider me to be a conversation partner. Over the next four weeks, we will discuss the primary crisis of our day, irresponsible individualism, and the need to shift the philosophical and theological emphases of our society. During the first two weeks our conversation will focus on philosophical and political issues, leaving the last two weeks for a discussion on theological and ecclesial matters.

This book is divided into four chapters with five essays in each chapter. After reading a chapter, you should visit the companion website, *RinR.org*, for a more interactive experience. With respect to the book's format, the reader is encouraged to go through one essay each day of the work week. Each day you read an essay, share your reflections about the essay with others. Each essay begins with a biblical proverb or passage to demonstrate that ancient wisdom has modern relevance. We need to connect the past to the present for a better future. In order to truly benefit from this conversation, you should join a social networking group, a weekend reading club, or a Sunday school class in order to share your ideas with others. The questions at the end of the essays are there to stimulate a variety of opinions, and the one sentence summary should enable you to articulate the salient points of each essay in your own words. Finally, it serves no purpose to discuss problems without presenting possible solutions. For that reason, the last essay will present a series of concepts and challenges that have the potential to bring about positive and lasting change, but that change will not come without a reformation in the hearts and minds of the people of the United States that leads to a Reformation in Responsibility.

Fourth Sunday of Advent, 2011

Chapter One:

The Perfect Philosophical Storm

Clearly, a majority of Americans are frustrated about the direction our nation is going. Our frustration is understandable. Just over two hundred years ago, we fought to overthrow a dictatorial government and over taxation. Now, many of our political leaders embrace government over-involvement (e.g. health care, the forced redistribution of wealth, the education of children, etc.) and over taxation (e.g. "increased revenue"). A hundred years ago, Christianity was the basis for American cultural values. Now, many of our leaders and entertainers push Christian values into the closet while vigorously promoting the Lesbian, Gay, Bi-sexual, and Transgender, hereafter LGBT, agenda. Fifty years ago, we had the strongest economy in the world. Now, we have accumulated an almost insurmountable national debt, and we are faced with the possibility of a catastrophic economic crisis within the decade. How did we change so quickly? Answer: Our civil philosophy and theology is responsible for our rapid change or better said—our rapid demise.

To avoid any misunderstandings this early in our conversation, let's state three things for the record: 1) promoting and protecting the rights of individuals is important for any society; 2) reason and science have provided tremendous benefits to our lives and culture and; 3) things do evolve, but not necessarily to the degree that many scientists would have us believe. With that said, the next five essays will discuss the fact that individualism, reason/science, and evolutionary thought have combined to form the perfect philosophical storm. These three aspects of modern philosophy have produced an extremely arrogant and socially counterproductive system of thought. As we discuss these philosophies, of primary concern is the danger they present to us. Thus, this work risks being overly negative, but it's a necessary risk in order to help our society reform. After reading this chapter, you will understand that our current crisis should come as no surprise. Our crisis is the logical result of our philosophies and policies.

Essay 1
The Rise of Individualism

Proverbs 18:1 – The one who lives alone is self-indulgent, showing contempt for all who have sound judgment.(NRSV)

The shift in thinking from the Medieval Period to the Renaissance and Enlightenment is important to understand because it involves the rise of individualism as the dominant ideology in the West. During the Medieval Period, there was no such thing as the social mobility that we know today. In Medieval Europe, the individual was expected to do his/her part for the good of the larger community. It has been said of that time, "there was a place for everyone, and everyone had a place." The focal points for a medieval community were the lord and/or lady and the estate. During the Renaissance and Enlightenment, the ideological emphasis began to shift away from the power holders toward the masses. Rooted in a sense of justice, Western philosophy started to emphasize the rights and values of all people regardless of social status. It was the beginning of a new era. It was the rise of individualism.

The term "individualism" has a variety of nuances. For purposes of this work, the term is used to refer to the value, protection, and promotion of the rights and beliefs of the individual. That's a good thing. Each individual should be valued in a society. Yet, when we talk about protecting the individual, a valid question is raised, namely: "From what does the individual need to be protected?" In answering this question, we begin to understand the dominant philosophy that drives our modern sense of justice in the West. Our civil philosophy and sense of justice demand that the rights and beliefs of the individual must be protected against the rights and beliefs of the majority. Now, from one perspective this is very logical and necessary for a just society. If you don't give some type of protection to the individual or minority group, then the majority will simply outvote them and nullify any influence a dissenting individual or minority group might have in society. Yet, from another perspective, the unchecked promotion of individual rights can be incredibly damaging to a society because the majority opinion is intentionally suppressed in order to let the minority opinion be expressed. Such a promotion of individualism first manifests itself in the expectation that the larger society should adapt for the individual, but the individual is not expected to adapt to the larger society. A second and even more disastrous manifestation is a complete cultural shift of morals and responsibilities in which the values and opinions of the minority are forced upon the majority by the courts. When this happens on a regular basis over the course of centuries, not only does the majority opinion become subservient to the individual/minority opinion in the courtroom, the majority opinion actually loses its influence over the larger society. This is what has happened in the United States, and this is what is destroying our nation. Our unchecked promotion of individual rights has evolved into an expression of irresponsible individualism.

Considering the fact that the U.S. was formed during the Enlightenment Period, it should come as no surprise that our nation embodies the philosophies and pursuits of that era. Yet, it also embodies the inherent dangers of the Enlightenment Period, namely, an overemphasis on the individual. It's absolutely essential to understand that one of the principal goals of many contemporary secularists is the empowerment of the minority opinion and the subjugation of the majority opinion. This goal isn't rooted in some national or global conspiracy theory. Rather, the goal of protecting and promoting the individual/minority opinion is rooted in the naïve belief that protecting the minority opinion from the majority opinion is the true expression of democratic justice. Our blind commitment to irresponsible individualism works like this—since defending the individual/minority opinion was clearly the right decision at some points in our history (e.g. the abolition of slavery, women's rights, the Civil Rights movement), then it must be the right decision all the time (e.g. financial aid for illegal aliens, the promotion of the LGBT agenda, supporting polygamous marriage, the promotion of Islam in the West, etc.). Ironically, this approach to individual rights is incredibly narrow-minded and anti-intellectual even though it is embraced by many who perceive themselves as intellectuals.

A recent example of the thoughtless pursuit of irresponsible individualism is depicted in the legal action being taken by the polygamists portrayed in the TV show, "Sister Wives." Their attorney, Jonathan Turley, states on his blog dated July 13, 2011:

> We are not demanding the recognition of polygamous marriage. We are only challenging the right of the state to prosecute people for their private relations... In that sense, the challenge is designed to benefit not just polygamists but all citizens who wish to live their lives according to their own values—even if those values run counter to those of the majority in the state.

Did you catch the last section of the quote? In the name of

justice and freedom, the courts are being used to suppress the values of the majority. This has been going on for decades, but hardly anyone challenges it because we have been taught that this is how a democracy works. Under the current system of thought, it's an injustice to offend an individual or minority group, in this case polygamists, but it's proper to promote values and opinions that "run counter to those of the majority" regardless of how many people are offended. That's not a democracy. That's irresponsible individualism. Ironically, irresponsible individualism is the greater injustice because it offends the majority of a nation's citizens. You see, irresponsible individualism doesn't dominate our society because it's synonymous with justice. It dominates our society because the majority have failed to stand up for their beliefs. For over a century now, many of our leading thinkers, politicians, and judges have been aggressive in their protection and promotion of the beliefs and values of the minority opinion while at the same time vehemently opposing the beliefs and values of the majority of our citizens. This is the reason, not in part but in whole, that America has changed so quickly with respect to its beliefs and values. What else would you expect when our leaders deliberately work against the beliefs and values of the majority of our people? The next time you hear people say they're frustrated because they don't know why our nation has changed so much, set them straight. Tell them why we've changed. Tell them it's the result of leaders who have convinced the majority that they must, in the name of democracy and justice, submit their beliefs and values to the minority opinion, but be sure to tell them that's an illogical lie. It's the lie of irresponsible individualism.

 Finally, there is a bitter paradox in all of this that was alluded to in the previous paragraph. Our leaders and philosophers have forgotten that a majority is not an entity in itself. A majority is, in substance, no different than a minority—both are collections of individuals. The only difference is that one collection happens to be larger than the other. Paradoxically, we protect small groups of individuals and we offend much larger groups of individuals. This is why, in our upside down society, it's a cardinal sin to offend an individual or a minority group, but it's perfectly acceptable to trample the values of the majority. Americans have been brainwashed into thinking that justice demands a suppression of the majority opinion in order to oblige the minority opinion. Make no mistake about it, irresponsible individualism is a societal cancer, and it will destroy our country if the majority does not stand against it.

Questions for Reflection:

What is your initial reaction to this essay?

What did you agree/disagree with in this essay? Why?

Have you ever witnessed the suppression of a majority opinion in order to promote a minority opinion? If so, describe the situation.

My summary of this essay:

Essay 2
The Query of Evolution

Psalm 14:1; 53:1 – The fool has said in his heart, "There is no God."(NKJV)

A creation account, whether it is a religious story recorded in a sacred text or a secular story recorded in a textbook, cannot be verified; both are propositions rooted in faith. For that reason, when a Christian evangelist holds a seminar in order to scientifically prove the creation account in Genesis, he looks more than a little out of place. He looks like a person trying to play baseball with a football. The rules and tools don't fit the game. A discussion of origins goes beyond the limits of science. There is no way to prove anything that happened 6,000 years ago let alone 6 million years ago. We may surmise about the origin of things or present an educated theory on origins, but we can never prove our position on origins. A discussion of origins, regardless of whether it is based in philosophy, theology, or science, is always a discussion rooted in faith.

All our finite human minds can adequately comprehend is the reality that something ordered the world we live in. Of course, atheists will balk at that statement, but isn't that what they're saying when they talk about evolution? There has to be a process behind the order around us. Something had to put the world in which we live into motion. For atheists and many agnostics, the order came about through a providential explosion that enabled the process of evolution to begin. However, if you pause and think about it, the theory of evolution never addresses the essential question of origins. Where did the exploding sun that resulted in the "Big Bang" come from? Theories that attempt to explain the evolutionary process are often presented, but unless those theories address the first elements in the universe, then they never address the essential question. Let's get right to the essential question. From where did the first elements come? From where did the universe come? Simply pushing the timetable back further and further, as evolutionary thought is accustomed to doing, provides no answer at all.

The answer to the question of origins can only be pursued in the realm of philosophy and theology. Here's an important question with which to begin: "Can something come from nothing?" Can you have absolute non-existence, nothingness, and then have something appear? Philosophically, that's not possible. It goes against everything we know. So then, the theist, the agnostic, and the atheist are presented with the same question, namely; "who or what stands at the very beginning of everything?" That's precisely the issue with which you need to wrestle in order to understand why theism has always been the dominant worldview. Even the philosophers of ancient Greece understood this dilemma. They used terms such as the "first cause" or the "unmoved mover" to refer to the essence that started everything. The first cause is that from which all other effects result. Yet, for the critical thinker this raises another question: "From where did the first cause originate?" Now, we are back to square one.

Was the first cause created? Did the first cause come from nothing? The former inquiry falls short because if it was created, then you're no longer dealing with the first cause. The latter approach won't work because, as we said earlier, it is a philosophical impossibility. Some philosophers and theologians of the ancient world acknowledged a third option that many in our era have forgotten. They believed that the first cause started or moved everything into motion. However, by nature of being the first cause, nothing could have started it or put it into motion. Thus, the first cause has always been and always will be. It is a perfect force that exists within itself and from which everything else finds its origin. Indeed, it is the "unmoved mover." At this point we have not determined by any means who or what the unmoved mover is, but we have certainly brought into question the foolishness of arguing the finer points of the creation and/or evolution of mundane things while avoiding the real dilemma of origins altogether.

> *The theist, the agnostic, and the atheist are presented with the same question, namely; "who or what stands at the very beginning of everything?"*

In addition to avoiding the essential question of origins, another problem with evolutionary thought is the fact that it is a self-promoting system. It essentially teaches that we're the best the world has ever seen. Sure, most evolutionists will argue that human beings will continue to evolve and get better, but that does not negate the fact that they think we are the best thus far. Whether or not we are better than those humans who have gone before us is something that is certainly up for debate. Although we've made great advances in science, the people of the ancient world had a better understanding than we do of many things (organic agriculture, the effects of the seasons of the year, natural healing remedies, etc.). The fact that theism dominated the ancient world demonstrates that some ancient perspectives are more plausible than modern perspectives—at least they were humble enough to believe that something ordered our world. On the other hand, we pride ourselves on our miniscule accomplishments, and we look right past the beautiful complexity of the created order around us. For example, consider a soldier who has lost a hand and has a robotic prosthetic. We stand amazed while watching a robotic hand work via sensors that monitor muscle movement in the forearm, yet we give little or no thought to the creator of the natural arm which is infinitely more complex than the prosthetic. Imagine if someone tried to convince us that the robotic arm was never designed but rather evolved over time. We would laugh that concept to scorn, but how many people accept the foolish argument that the natural arm was never designed even though it is infinitely more complex than the robotic arm? Undoubtedly, we should celebrate the amazing technology that goes into prosthetics today, but we should be even more amazed at how we are "fearfully and wonderfully made."

Here's another example of the philosophical necessity of creation; imagine that you are walking through the Sahara Desert and you come across an aquarium. As you look at the aquarium, you notice that the fish inside are healthy, the inside of the aquarium is decorated with vegetation, and there is a battery operated oxygenator attached to tank. Knowing that fish don't live in a desert, you immediately deduce that these fish have a caretaker evidenced by the fact that their lives are sustained by an environment designed just for their well being (i.e. the aquarium) in the midst of a much larger and incredibly inhospitable environment (i.e. the Sahara Desert). In this scenario you know that life exists beyond the desert, but you also know that fish cannot live in the desert. Would anyone in his right mind attribute the aquarium's existence to an evolutionary process? Again, such a proposition would be comically irrational. Yet, the same truths that are evident in this illustration are also evident in our universe. Undoubtedly, there is life out there somewhere, but as far as we have looked into the universe, the closest planet that might sustain life as we know it is roughly 600 light years away. For all practical purposes, our universe is a biological desert. Our earth is the aquarium. We are the fish. In the midst of an incredibly inhospitable universe, this world was perfectly designed for our well being. It is beyond reason to dismiss the fact that we have a Caretaker.

Contrary to contemporary belief, the Bible presents one of the most compelling philosophical arguments for understanding the origins of our universe. The name of God, I AM, depicted in Exodus 3:14 and the biblical concept of God being the, "Alpha and Omega" (the first and last letters of the Greek alphabet), both imply that the Divine Essence has no beginning or end. The Divine Essence is the beginning and end of all things. In the New Testament, the opening statement of the fourth gospel says, "In the beginning was the Word and the Word was with God and the Word was God." (NKJV) Rendered another way, "At the origin of all things, was the Divine Essence and the Divine Essence was with God and the Divine Essence was God." Let it suffice to say that part of a Reformation in Responsibility involves the humility to admit three things: 1) it's irrational to deny that something has ordered our world; 2) it's immature to think that we are better than those who have gone before us and; 3) it's irresponsible to glorify our own work and dismiss the work of God.

Questions for Reflection:
What is your initial reaction to this essay?

What did you agree/disagree with in this essay? Why?

Do you think the aquarium-in-the-desert analogy is plausible? Why or why not?

My summary of this essay:

Essay 3
The Modern Scientific Error

Proverbs 16:18 – Pride goes before destruction, and a haughty spirit before a fall.(NKJV)

Ironically, one of the most significant literary contributions of the Enlightenment Period was Thomas Paine's (1737-1809) famous work, *The Age of Reason*. Paine's title reflected the sentiments of the age. Reason was the way of the future. Religious faith was the way of fools. As the Enlightenment gave way to the Industrial Revolution and the latter gave way to the modern scientific era, sharp distinctions were made between faith and reason, church and state, religious and secular. Over time, the Church gave up its place as the dominant influence on Western society, and today the dominant influence in the West is a peculiar blend of agnosticism and secularism. Yet, the arrogant notion that our era is superior to previous eras because we live by reason is the great fiction of our time and the source of many of our societal failures.

Before going any further, it's important to clarify some terms that we're using. For purposes of this work, "faith" is defined as belief that is not based in proof. Most of us would agree that "faithful" is a good term for a religious worldview, since such a worldview cannot be proven—at least not yet. This brings us to the term "proof." Proof is evidence that a given thing is true. Most of us would agree that a scientific worldview seeks proof, that is, a scientist uses various methods of analysis to ensure that what he or she is committing to is indeed true. However, what if it's not? What if a scientist's conclusions are wrong in the end? Should the scientist be considered a person of reason or a person of faith? Many would argue that the scientist should be considered a person of reason because, at the very least, he/she sought proof for his/her conclusions despite the fact that they were wrong. However, there is another perspective to consider. Proof leads to truth. This brings us to the question of the ages, which is captured in the words of Pontius Pilate (John 18:38); "What is truth?" Truth is the verification and/or validation that a given thing is corrrect. Thus, if a scientist believes in something that is later proven to be false, then the scientist's belief wasn't rooted in proof. Regardless of how scientific a proposition may sound, if it does not lead to truth, then it was not grounded in proof. Rather, it was grounded in faith. Remember, faith is belief in something that cannot be proven—at least not yet. Here's some proof—during the last century, scientists have flip-flopped on more conclusions than politicians. Here's the truth—every time science disproves science, it proves that faith is as much a part of science as it is a part of religion.

In January of 2000, I considered continuing my studies at Oxford University. Part of the process involved an interview with a potential advisor. During our conversation, the professor made a remark that has stuck with me. He said, "Americans often think they know more than they do." Arguably, he was right, but that's not just an American error. It's the modern scientific error. Our technological accomplishments have given us a false sense of certitude. Less than fifty years ago, people travelled to the moon. Daily, an international space station is staffed by a multinational crew. Modern medicine has conquered many diseases that were fatal in the past. We are able to communicate faster and over further distances than ever before—and the list could go on and on. These and other accomplishments are certainly worth celebrating and should be improved upon. We should continue to explore our galaxy. We should seek to increase the quality and average length of human life. One day, we should colonize the moon. Someday soon, we should send humans to Mars. Prayerfully, we'll find a cure for cancer. Yet, all of these things should be pursued with a great sense of humility, which is something we desperately lack.

> *The thinking of our era is so environmentally and socially destructive that a Reformation in Responsibility demands that we alter it.*

Reason and science have clearly won the hearts and minds of our leaders and intellectuals, but when we step back and look at the big picture, all of our advances have come at a very high price. We fought two devastating World Wars, but we keep on fighting. We watch oil spills destroy our oceans, but we drill deeper. What is responsible for this destruction? Is religion responsible? I've often heard people say something to the effect of, "More wars have been fought in the name of religion than anything else." That may be true as you add up the wars that have been fought over the centuries, but more people have been killed during the "age of reason" than in all the other ages put together. What about the ecosystem? Is religion also responsible for the destruction of our environment? Now, don't misunderstand what I'm saying. Science has provided the modern era with tremendous benefits, but a harsh reality is that science, not religion, is the most destructive force the world has ever seen. This truth infuriates secularists as they are being forced to defend what is becoming an indefensible position, namely, that reason and science have made us better people. The truth is, the

Age of Reason has been more painful than Thomas Paine ever imagined.

Harvard Professor Steven Pinker's recent publication *The Better Angels of Our Nature: Why Violence Has Declined*, is a perfect example of the modern secularist dilemma. Pinker acknowledges the wars and atrocities of the 20th century, but he goes on to argue that, if you look at the number of violent deaths per capita, the 20th century was actually the most peaceful century on record. The fact that Pinker needs a research team and hundreds of pages of charts and graphs to make his point proves that his point is really not worth making. The most powerful points are the ones that need little clarification. In reality, Pinker's book is not a new revelation based on solid research. Rather, his book is a biased display of secularism that seeds the clouds of the perfect philosophical storm. Predictably, Pinker dates the significant shift in human nonviolence to the Enlightenment Period and the rise of reason and science with result of our newfound intelligence being the most peaceful and enlightened era in human history. Anyone with common sense knows that we made a mess of the 20th century, but, for reasons that will be discussed in Essay 5, secularists like Pinker despise common sense. Despite the enormous effort on the part of secularists to defend the superiority of the Enlightenment Period and the advance of reason and science, in the millennia to come, our era may actually go down in the record books as one of the most unreasonable, destructive, and arrogant eras in history.

Our era does not want to face the reality that there aren't enough facts to enable us to live by facts alone. There is no such thing as an age of faith, an age of reason, a person of faith, or a person of reason. Everyone lives by faith. It is impossible to separate faith and reason from one another.

Yet, the 20th century made an impressive and ignoble attempt at doing just that, and the result was a series of tragic failures. We must embrace the fact that faith and reason are mutually dependent and are a part of every human experience. We are finite beings. In varying measures, faith and reason are a part of every person, every family, every nation, and every era. Thus, there is little difference between religious surety and scientific surety—both are naïve.

In closing, the term secular is the perfect word to describe the dominant thinking of our day. The term, like most terms, has a number of nuances. It can be used to describe worldliness, temporality, or something that is limited to a specific age. Our era fits each nuance of the term. Our society is incredibly shortsighted with little ability to look beyond the passing pleasures of this life. The decisions we make are driven by temporal concerns that have little relevance for the next few decades, let alone for centuries, for millennia, or for eternity. Finally, the thinking of our era is so environmentally and socially destructive that a Reformation in Responsibility demands that we alter it, thus fulfilling a self-titled prediction, namely, that secularism and irresponsible individualism should be limited to this age—The Age of Foolishness.

Questions for Reflection:
What is your initial reaction to this essay?

What did you agree/disagree with in this essay? Why?

What are your thoughts about the successes and failures of the 20th century?

My summary of this essay:

Essay 4
Life, Liberty, & the Pursuit of Unhappiness

Proverbs 14:12; 16:25 – "*There is a way that seems right to a man, but in the end it leads to death.*"(NIV)

It was November of 2005. I was going through some e-mails when I received some incredibly sobering news. A former classmate from The Citadel, who was no longer in the military, passed away. I didn't know the circumstances, but as I sat processing the e-mail that November day, I couldn't help but think—just thirteen years ago, in May of 1992, we graduated with the world at our fingers. How did this happen? In the days ahead, another Citadel classmate told me the sad circumstances surrounding our friend's passing. He had contracted AIDS and, toward the end of his life, he was living in incredibly humble conditions in West Hollywood. His life was filled with talent and potential and, in a bitter irony, it was brought to ruin in a place renowned for talent and potential. There's no doubt that Hollywood is filled with people who have everything this world has to offer, beauty, notoriety, wealth, power—yet so many of them are empty. Could there be a greater paradox? Whenever I see the iconic Hollywood Sign, I think of my former classmate and the sad lesson Hollywood teaches us—the pursuit of happiness will never make you happy.

So, how do we find happiness? The second sentence of our Declaration of Independence, when it is understood properly, is a positive expression of individualism and a key to finding happiness. "We hold these truths to be self-evident, that all men are created equal, that they are endowed by their Creator with certain unalienable rights, that among these are life, liberty and the pursuit of happiness." Here are the great truths of our independence succinctly stated. All human beings are "created equal" and "endowed by their Creator with certain unalienable rights." The primary rights the Creator has given us apply to life, liberty, and the pursuit of happiness. Yet, we have come to a place where majority values and civil religion have been challenged and opposed so effectively by social engineers and activist judges that, in the name of individual rights, we have actually undermined our Declaration of Independence. To understand this dilemma, let's work our way back from our three primary rights to the source of those rights.

> *The pursuit of happiness will never make you happy.*

First, let's consider the right to pursue happiness. Do you really think the intention of our early leaders was to use the power of the state to support socially dysfunctional lifestyles under the guise of a person's pursuit of happiness? Obviously, many secularists and liberals believe just that as they are fond of saying that a person has the right to "pursue happiness as he or she defines it." That's quite a philosophical stroke of the brush. Where does such a pursuit end? Well, it ends with the pursuit of traditional values. From the secularist and liberal perspective, it seems that this wide open pursuit of happiness-as-you-define-it only applies to individuals and minorities that don't agree with traditional values. For example, if one defines happiness as the ability for one's children to make their way through society without being coerced to accept the validity of homosexuality or same-sex marriage, then the courts expect you to be unhappy. If you are offended that, in order to accommodate non-traditional families, the terms "mother" and "father" are replaced with "Parent 1" and "Parent 2" on the new U.S. Passport forms, then secularists expect you to deal with it. Let's redefine marriage, motherhood, and fatherhood, in order to accommodate the happiness of a miniscule percentage of the population. That's not right. That's not democratic. That's a classic example of irresponsible individualism. However, if a large segment of the population is unhappy about the fact that the civil religion of the country is marginalized by the government, the courts don't consider that worth worrying about. To the contrary, it is something to worry about because a true democracy listens to the concerns of all people, not just the concerns of minority groups.

Second, let's critique the American concept of liberty and the right of the people to live out their conscience, which is somewhat of a myth in our society. The public school system is a classic example of our loss of liberty. In our "free" society, a public school system in the Bible Belt that's overwhelmingly comprised of Christian families, Christian educators, and Christian administrators does not have the right to introduce any aspect of religion into the daily routine of the students and faculty. The basis for the elimination of religion from the public schools is the argument of separation of church and state. Interestingly, the argument's original intent was to prevent a state run church as was common in Europe, but it has evolved into a separation of the popular religion of the people and the state. How do we know that the original intent is not what is being enforced today? Answer: The founders and early leaders of our country never applied the constitutional interpretations that contemporary lawyers and judges are applying to our society today (more on this in Essays 6 & 19). Let's return to our example of a public school in the Bible Belt. If you promote Christianity in a public school system in the South, there is no doubt that you will be forcing someone who pays taxes to put up with something they don't profess or believe. That is not to say that you are forcing them to practice Christianity. However, you are forcing them to accept the fact that the majority will be exercising their right to pray and practice their religion as Christians. No doubt some would argue that this is a constitutional violation because the non-Christian minorities involved are offended by what is taking place at a tax-sponsored institution. Yet, there is another side to the argument. What about 90% of the families in the school system who believe in Christianity and would love to see it as a formal part of the school day? Aren't they tax payers? What about the public schools promotion of homosexuality which runs counter to the beliefs of orthodox Christianity? If the government believes that one tax-paying minority family in the Bible Belt should not have to put up with the beliefs of Christianity, why does the government believe that the majority of tax-paying Christians in the Bible Belt should have to put up with the beliefs of the minority? Answer: The courts and the secularists leading our government are naively convinced this is justice, and we the people have foolishly accepted their naiveté. Liberty demands that communities be allowed to decide for themselves how they will educate their children and how they will assimilate their religious beliefs into their public lives.

Third, we must give our attention to the right to life. The loss of the right to life is captured in one word, abortion. There is no need to throw out statistics on abortion. You can go online and find hundreds of statistics on your own. The fact is, with the number of abortions that take place in

America annually, it is clear that the majority of abortions in our country are for the sake of convenience not because the life of the mother or child is in danger. Furthermore, it comes as no surprise that the states that consistently rank among the highest percentage of abortions are states that most reflect secularism and irresponsible individualism (e.g. California). It's amazing that our society idolizes California. The state is bankrupt in every way—morally, economically, environmentally, and with respect to its political leadership. Warning to the reader, the philosophies and decisions that govern California will never lead to success. Rather than finding happiness, California is blue for a reason—pun intended.

Finally, it should come as no surprise that the erosion of our freedoms involves an attack on the very source of our freedom, that is, an attack on God. With the elimination of God from our civil conscience, we've initiated a process of rapid decline. Take away one's sense of responsibility to God, and one's sense of responsibility to family and society will be the next to fall to the wayside. For this reason, the Bible teaches that our relationships with one another are in large part determined by our relationships with God (Matthew 22:35-40). Thomas Jefferson is known for saying, "It does me no injury for my neighbor to say there are twenty gods, or no God. It neither picks my pocket nor breaks my leg." Actually, it does. Your neighbor's theology, or lack of, will have a direct impact on how he/she fulfills his/her responsibilities to society. A Reformation in Responsibility involves standing up for our rights to life and liberty, but we need to understand that the blind pursuit of happiness will never make us happy. In order to be happy, we must first fulfill our responsibilities to God, family, and society—a point that will be discussed further in Essay 17.

Questions for Reflection:
What is your initial reaction to this essay?

What did you agree/disagree with in this essay? Why?

When you think of the happiest times in your life, what is it that made you happy? How does your pursuit of happiness square with this essay?

My summary of this essay:

Essay 5
Adolescent America

Proverbs 30:11-13 – There is a generation that curses its father, and does not bless its mother. There is a generation that is pure in its own eyes, yet is not washed from its filthiness. There is a generation—oh, how lofty are their eyes... (NKJV)

At some point, all of us have come in contact with a rebellious young person who knows better than all the adults in his or her life. In part, the rebellion of youth is natural. During the transition to adulthood, a person should gain a sense of independence. Indeed, there is a necessary sense of empowerment that comes with adolescence. Yet, this transition is often accompanied by an immature attitude toward one's elders. One of the hallmarks of maturity is a genuine appreciation for those people who helped form and co-construct one's identity in a positive way. Conversely, hallmarks of adolescent immaturity include but are not limited to, a lack of respect for one's elders, an inability to see the wisdom that comes with age and experience, and an inability to see the inadequacy of unilateral decision making. Compared to these hallmarks of adolescence, our nation is acting like an adolescent on the global scene.

Established less than 300 years ago, we are teenagers among the empires and dynasties of world history. The Egyptian dynasties lasted well over 2,000 years. Rome had a 500 year republic and a 400 year empire. Boasting that we are the greatest nation in the history of the world is not only less than factual; it's the height of arrogance. Even in the midst of a debt crisis, some economists and politicians still claim that we have the strongest economy the world has ever seen. How can any thinking person who is knowledgeable of history take a comment like that seriously? Like an unruly adolescent, our society makes things difficult for itself by ignoring the sound advice of societies that have gone before us. Our culture ignores this advice because we are convinced that we are better than those who've gone before us. The United States has had money, power, and prestige, all in a very short period of time, but due to the self-centered and adolescent philosophies that drive our society, "Adolescent America" is quickly losing each of them.

Our nation is like a dysfunctional home where the attitudes and actions of the adolescents determine the agenda while the paralyzed parents of religion and traditional values sit back wondering what they can or should do. If people in our society who respect God and traditional values do not stand up in the decades ahead, our nation will fall. This isn't prophetic; it's common sense. Like rebellious teenagers, our stubbornness and shortsightedness is resulting in our demise. Indeed, the perfect philosophical storm of individualism, reason/science, and evolutionary thought drives the adolescent attitude of secular Americans. Evolution teaches us that we are the most advanced generation that has ever walked the earth. Reason and science have convinced us that we are the smartest generation that has ever walked the earth, and irresponsible individualism places each person's desires above the needs of the larger society. In short, we have educated a generation of narcissists who have little to no respect for the beliefs and traditions of the generations that have preceded us. We mock theology and the traditional family values that have been cherished by the overwhelming majority of people who have gone before us. Yet, our arrogance has blinded us to the fact that our era is the most unstable and destructive era in human history.

This arrogance also explains why secularists consistently reject common sense. Secularists really believe that we are so advanced and so reasonable that the logic and rules of the past are no longer applicable to us. In a way, it is as if the minority of people who live in the present are defiantly waving their fists toward the majority who have lived in the past. The vast majority of people in the past embraced some form of theism. Thus, we reject theism. All societies before us shared the same family structure, namely, men and women coming together in marriage in order to establish a family. Thus, we challenge the traditional family. Generations before us saw debt as a hindrance to success. Thus, we promote debt as the way forward. Common sense was once respected and valued. Thus, we take every opportunity to prove common sense wrong.

Secularists and liberals can't appreciate that which is common because they don't want to be common. Secularists love to feel superior to the masses. They want to believe that their way of thinking is superior to the common sense of the people. To prove their point, secularists often complicate common sense matters with a few obscure facts, even though those facts may be completely erroneous, in an attempt to make reasonable people feel inferior. Our financial crisis is a classic example. Consumers can't get in the habit of spending more than they make—full stop. If they try to ignore that bit of common sense it will catch up with them. Yet, it is common to find economists and politicians who will argue that more debt will actually help in the end. Accumulating debt will not lead to financial success. It won't work. It can't work—you take that to the bank. Furthermore, deliberately challenging the sentiments of the average American through popular

TV programs and commercial advertisements is one of the primary ways secularists start the process of making people more tolerant of that which was not tolerated in the past. This is what has happened with the issue of homosexuality over the last four decades. This is what has been happening with Islam since 9/11. This is what has just begun with the issue of polygamy. With respect to polygamy, Muslims not Mormons will be the real beneficiaries of the secularist/liberal agenda to promote polygamy. Nothing would be more pleasing to the liberal agenda than to erase our Judeo-Christian heritage and replace it with secularism, same-sex marriage, polygamy, and a good dose of Islam. But again, this agenda is not driven by a conspiracy theory. The agenda is driven by the naïve notion that democracy demands that we support the minority opinion over and against the majority opinion. Indeed, a good liberal would argue that traditional American history and our Christian heritage have little importance for modern America. As a matter of fact, liberals would prefer to establish a homosexual history month rather than discuss the role of Christianity in American history (e.g. California public schools and SB 48). In reality, traditional values and Christian history have never been more needed for the future success of America.

> *It's time for America to grow up and realize that God and society are not responsible to the individual. Individuals are responsible to God and society.*

Watching our nation right now is like watching a young person disregard the advice of her parents, throw off the shackles of traditional morality, and pursue happiness at all costs. All of us know how that will end. Regardless of whether or not she ever comes home, it will be a rough road ahead—and so it is with our nation. We have travelled so far down this road of social and economic irresponsibility that even the right decision to turn back will involve very difficult decisions for the future. Suffice it to say that reasonable and responsible households are those where adolescents contribute to the good of the home, not those where the entire home revolves around the desires of dysfunctional adolescents. It's time for America to get its house in order. Do we have the courage to follow through with such decisions? Only the future can give us the answer to that question. A Reformation in Responsibility involves restoring the importance of the majority opinion; refusing to borrow our way out of our problems; restoring a sense of personal responsibility to God, family, and society; rejecting government officials who promote irresponsible individualism; and finally, having the courage to stand up to government officials who have long rejected the traditional values of the majority. It's time for America to grow up and realize that God and society are not responsible to the individual. Individuals are responsible to God and society.

Questions for Reflection:
What is your initial reaction to this essay?

What did you agree/disagree with in this essay? Why?

Do you think the term "adolescent" is appropriate for describing the attitude of our nation? Why or why not?

My summary of this essay:

Chapter Two

The Separation Of Thought And State

The following chapter will no doubt offend many secularists and liberals because they have worked extremely hard to protect the separation of thought and state. As we discussed in the previous chapter, irresponsible individualism, arrogant evolutionary thought, and a blind devotion to reason/science have moved us along our current trajectory. There is no doubt that secularists and liberals have had an amazing impact on our society in the last century. In the name of justice, they disregard the rights of the majority of the population. In the name of increased revenue, they overtax people, especially the most productive people. In the name of wisdom, they abandon traditional values and common sense. And, in the name of education, they eliminate moral formation from the public schools. All of these decisions are the result of senseless secularism. Yet, liberal secularism will do significantly more damage if it is not opposed.

In the next five essays we will address the following issues: 1) the courts reluctance to support the traditional or majority opinion; 2) the never ending problem of greed and taxation; 3) the role of marriage in society; 4) the essence of education; and 5) our current state of confusion. If one spends any amount of time in higher education, one quickly learns that complicating simple truths is something many secularists have mastered. When a secularist realizes that he or she is losing an argument, he/she usually makes one of the following comments: "I think we need to find a compromise on this;" or "the issue is more complicated than that." The former is usually an attempt at preventing any further loss or embarrassment in order to regroup and come back to the argument another day. The latter is usually an indication that you are frustrating them with those meddlesome things called facts. Don't get me wrong. Some things are very complicated, and those who are inclined toward critical thinking will more easily recognize those complexities. However, many secularists overcomplicate matters, not because the issues are actually complicated, but because they don't want to believe like the majority. Proving the majority wrong provides them with a personal sense of superiority.

Another point to consider is that many people are persuaded by perception more than by fact. The ancient Greeks used to say that there are three key aspects to persuasive public speaking: *logos*, which is the content of what is being said; *pathos*, which is the speaker's passion for what is being said; and *ethos*, which is the perceived credibility of the speaker in the minds of the listeners. Interestingly, the Greeks used to say that *ethos* was the most important aspect of persuasive public speaking. That is still the case today. Sure, what is being said should be the most important, but in reality, people are persuaded more by their perceptions than by the facts presented to them. For example, a secularist will respect the unnecessarily complicated views of an Ivy League economist simply because of the perception of intellectualism and research that comes with the Ivy League. Yet, the same secularist will dismiss the simplistic views of a person with financial common sense because he/she lacks any intellectual persona. The same is true on environmental issues, sexuality, marriage, etc. It's an insane game that secularists play, but they know the playing field well enough to win, which is what they have been doing for the last century. The goal of this chapter is to level the playing field by presenting simple but solid principles to oppose liberal secularism and reform our social, financial, and educational priorities and responsibilities.

Essay 6
A Government of the Courts for the Minority

Proverbs 14:28 – In a multitude of people is a king's honor, but in the lack of people is the downfall of a prince. (NKJV)

Here's an example of how blind many of our people and leaders have become in the United States. When we are promoting democracy in other parts of the world (e.g. the Middle East), and we realize that the majority vote of the people is less than favorable to our interests, that is, if the Palestinians vote in Hamas or the Egyptians vote in the Muslim Brotherhood or Libya and Tunisia vote in Islamic governments, then the typical response from secularist American leaders is either: 1) part of a democratic process is dealing with outcomes that we do not like; or 2) the election was rigged and is therefore not a reflection of democracy. However, when it comes to the people of California passing Proposition 8 and voting down same sex marriage, well, that's a different story. In the case of Proposition 8, liberals and secularists are: 1) unwilling to deal with such a vote as they are quick to claim that prohibiting same-sex marriage is an unconstitutional and undemocratic violation of human rights; and 2) willing to strike down the vote of the people by the decision of one person, namely, one liberal judge. How hypocritical! That is not democracy! That is not a government of the people by the people and for the people. It's a government of the courts by the secularists for the minority. It's the highest form of American hypocrisy, and it's nothing short of a violation of majority rights. Remember, the majority, just like the minority, is made up of individuals. California, one of the most liberal states in the country, could not pass same-sex marriage with a straight, no pun intended, up or down vote. The only way same sex marriage will be accepted by the American people is if the government forces them to accept it, and that's exactly what's happening. Same-sex marriage is not the people's choice. Same-sex marriage is being forced on the people via the courts and the public education system, and amazingly the majority stands by and does little more than try to play by the rules of a system that is manipulated by liberal secularists.

Here's a shocking example of how skewed the western concept of justice has become. Recently, a judge in the United Kingdom ruled in favor of a homosexual couple who sued a heterosexual Christian couple because they were refused a room in the latter's privately owned bed and breakfast. On what grounds can a judge make such a ruling? A rationale is set forth by Chai Feldblum, a member of the U.S. Equal Employment Opportunity Commission, in an essay titled, "Moral Conflict and Liberty: Gay Rights and Religion," (2006).

> "…for all my sympathy for the evangelical Christian couple who may wish to run a bed and breakfast from which they can exclude unmarried, straight couples and all gay couples, this is a point where I believe the "zero sum" nature of the game inevitably comes into play… I am convinced that society should come down on the side of protecting the liberty of LGBT people. Once individuals choose to enter the stream of economic commerce by opening commercial establishments, I believe it is legitimate to require that they play by certain rules. Just as we do not tolerate private racial beliefs that adversely affect African-Americans… we should not tolerate private beliefs… that adversely affect LGBT people. But that is not to say that we should not acknowledge that this zero-sum game has resulted in a burden on some individual's belief liberty

and that we not be forced to articulate why such a burden is appropriate."

Sadly, not only does Mrs. Feldblum acknowledge that she is willing to overlook the sentiments of the majority, she acknowledges that the majority's "belief liberty" should be burdened and that "such a burden is appropriate." However, changing words does not change concepts. People with common sense would call the concept of "burdening someone's liberty" by its more common name—"tyranny." Furthermore, Mrs. Feldblum's sentiments are an insult to the African-American community. She promotes the liberal and secular notion that morality, like ethnicity, is an issue that is beyond one's control. Part of Reformation in Responsibility involves the refusal to accept the argument that the Civil Rights movement, which was a noble cause, is identical in nature to the LGBT movement. Ethnicity and morality are not the same. Ethnicity is an issue that was determined before birth. Morality is an issue that is determined every day.

Mrs. Feldblum's radical views, which are the norm among lawmakers today, are found wanting on a number of points. First, she forces religion into the closet, insomuch as she essentially confines "religious beliefs" and "being religious" to religious rituals and gatherings. However, one of the primary goals of the religious life is to make a difference in the world. To say that running a business, in this case a guesthouse, is not a religious act and thus has no bearing on one's practice of

If secularist judges have their way, Christians will be able to say whatever they want, but only in their worship services. Their beliefs will not be allowed outside the church, not even in their privately owned businesses. In a civil and thinking society, this type of judicial tyranny should be opposed at all costs and with all measures.

religion reflects an ignorance of and insensitivity toward the essence of religion. For a religious person, what one does outside his/her place of worship is the real indicator as to whether or not he/she is actually a religious person.

To return to the recent court case in the U.K., the verdict found the Christian couple guilty of breaking the British equality law. The argument against the Christian couple is that religious freedom cannot be used as a justification for prejudice and an excuse to violate human rights. How does a judge find the Christian couple guilty of violating human rights? Undoubtedly, the Christian couple is discriminating against the homosexual community because their religious beliefs do not promote the practice of homosexuality. However, their refusal to provide accommodations for homosexuals or, as their policy stated, unmarried heterosexual couples is an act of passive discrimination, that is, the Christian couple is not telling the homosexual couple that they must adopt the beliefs and practices of Christianity. For all practical purposes there may be a homosexual motel across the street where the homosexual couple can find accommodations in a likeminded environment. Yet, the court's action in forcing the Christian couple to accomodate homosexuals is an act of aggressive discrimination and a flagrant violation of their human rights. Which is more unjust; asking people to leave your property because you don't agree with their lifestyle, or forcing people to accommodate a lifestyle with which they don't agree on their own private property? With certitude, one can proclaim the latter is the greater injustice and is an act of judicial tyranny. In an asinine decision the judge has, in the name of human rights, become the more grievous violator of human rights.

Sadly, the current judicial climate in Europe and America is more than willing to support such judicial tyranny and blatant disregard for the majority sentiment. In essence, secularists have wholeheartedly opened the door for the LGBT community to come out of the closet, while at the same time they have pushed Christianity into the closet, that is, the closet traditionally referred to as the church. If secularist judges have their way, Christians will be able to say whatever they want, but only in their worship services. Their beliefs will not be allowed outside the church, not even in their privately owned businesses. In a civil and thinking society, this type of judicial tyranny should be opposed at all costs and with all measures. If the courts feel they have the right to ignore the voice of the people, then it is only a matter of time before the people will begin to ignore the voice of the courts. When that time comes, the courts will have themselves to blame. A Reformation in Responsibility involves the end of judicial tyranny and the restoration of majority rights. For this to happen, the majority of our people will need the courage to stand up to a government of the courts by the secularists for the minority and say, "No!" The majority must restore the American concept of a government of the people by the people and for the people.

Questions for Reflection:
What is your initial reaction to this essay?

What did you agree/disagree with in this essay? Why?

What do you think is the proper role of the courts in our society? Do you think the courts are overstepping their boundaries? Explain your answers.

My summary of this essay:

Essay 7
TAXATION & ECONOMIC TYRANNY

Proverbs 15:27 – Greed brings grief to the whole family…^(NLT)

Taxes are inevitable, but they need to be managed for the good of the people. Raising taxes will never solve our nation's financial problems. It will only exacerbate them. Winston Churchill wisely stated that raising taxes in order to strengthen a nation's economy is "like a man standing in a bucket trying to lift himself up by the handle." In order for a nation to be strong, the people need to be strong. In order for the people to be strong, they need to keep the vast majority of their money in their pockets. In general, people who surrender the responsibility for their well being to the government are a people who are destined to be robbed by their government via taxation. For example, those in the highest tax bracket are taxed nearly 40% of their income. However, when you add all their taxes together (income, social security, medicare/medicaid, property, vehicle, gas, sales, utilities, etc.) those people are taxed on nearly 50% of their earned income. Furthermore, we are adding to our national debt at an irresponsible rate. From January 2009 until November 2011, our national debt has gone from roughly $10.7 trillion to just over $15 trillion. That's a 40% increase in just three years. If things do not change, then the average taxpayer's total taxation will be forced to roughly 40%. That's criminal. Regardless of what a government says about liberty, if that same government is taking roughly 40% of its average citizen's hard earned money, that government is oppressive.

No government can take close to half of a person's earnings and say their citizens are free. Additionally, no government can take that much money from its most productive people without destroying itself in the end. When pushed too far, visionary leaders and productive people will take their motivation and skills, the very things that made them productive, and go somewhere else. They'll put them to use in a place where the reward is worth the effort. That's precisely what has occurred with American industry. Under the guise of equality and labor laws, the government has put so many stipulations on American companies that our companies have simply gone overseas. Dismantling American industry provided a short term benefit to the government because people became more dependent on the government and less dependent on corporations. However, the long term consequences of increased entitlement programs and decreased American industry are disastrous. Those who live off the system provide very little, if anything, toward stabilizing the system. Thus, the current American system is destined to fail. Unless there is a significant reduction in government responsibility, the people of the United States will continue to live with excessive taxation precisely because there will never be enough "increased revenue" to pay for the decreased responsibility of our people. So, how do we stabilize the system?

It doesn't take a college degree to realize that a nation's financial success is proportionate to its industrial success (e.g. Britain in the 18th century, America in the 19th and 20th centuries, China in the 21st century). The sooner our country restores its industry, the better off our country will be. I was born in Schenectady, New York. In the 1960's and 1970's, Schenectady was a booming blue collar city that epitomized American strength and tenacity, but during the early 1990's

General Electric (GE) started pulling out of the city in order to relocate in South Carolina, a non-union state. Simply put, the union demands placed on GE proved to be more than the company was willing to tolerate. Labor laws and unions are a good thing if they are held in check. If the government and the unions demand more and more, then their demands will eventually destroy a business, a corporation, or a nation. Every time I drive through a once prosperous industrial city in the northeast or an abandoned mill town in the south, I shake my head in frustration. There's no doubt that our people, if they still had jobs, could produce a better product than the people of Indonesia or China, but government over-involvement in labor has destroyed American industry. When employers are forced to jump through economic hoops in order to employ Americans, the result is obvious. They won't employ Americans. They'll go overseas or employ migrant workers. However, don't make the naïve mistake of thinking that our financial crisis is a result of corporate greed alone. Individual greed, not corporate greed, is the driving force of the American society. It's important to understand that greed manifests itself through laziness and attitudes of entitlement as much as it manifests itself through big corporate bonuses.

From the person living off the public dole, to the union shop steward who's seeking more benefits, to the corporate executive who's making millions per week, Americans are controlled by their desires for the amenities of life and the perceived pleasures they bring. That should be no surprise since our primary goal is the "pursuit of happiness." Yet, our lust for money and pleasure is dismantling our economic and social foundations. In our pursuit of happiness, we have become so blinded by greed and pleasure that we are making utterly senseless decisions with our resources. For example, we have become the first society in the history of the world to consistently pay court jesters (athletes and entertainers) more money than philosophers, physicians, and kings (educators, doctors, and politicians). Why don't we see people protesting the millions of dollars being made by athletes and entertainers? At least a corporate CEO has the potential to provide thousands of jobs for a community. What does an athlete or an entertainer do for the larger society? Answer: athletes and entertainers are not protested because they provide exactly what modern America is always pursuing but never seems to find—happiness. In our foolish pursuit of happiness, we have watched our national debt go from roughly $4 trillion in 1990 to over $15 trillion in 2011. In two decades, our debt has increased over 275%! If America does not change its current financial course, then the next two decades will likely witness the failure of our financial system. Indeed, we are experiencing tyranny, but it's a tyranny from within.

A Reformation in Responsibility involves the restoration of American Industry and the understanding that people should keep the vast majority of their money in their pockets rather than in the government's coffers.

Yet, the decision that will likely go down as one of the top-ten most foolish decisions in world history is our decision to provide China with the platform for its economic growth. God forbid that we ever go to war with China, but if we do, we have our greed to thank for their ability to sustain their army on the battlefield. For decades China's military was never a threat because, although it was enormous in size, they never had the infrastructure to keep their military in the field. Now, thanks to the irresponsible greed of modern America, China can march her army around the world and sustain it on the battlefield for an indefinite period of time. In December 2010, I went back to Ft. Benning to pin Airborne Wings on a recent graduate of U.S. Army Airborne School. While I was there, I went to a local military supply store, and I was shocked at the number of military items that were marked, "Made in China." Undoubtedly, our decisions are comical to our competitors and enemies, but it's hard to laugh if you're an American. Next time you go to Wal-Mart, think about it. Would you rather have cheap socks or a secure job and national security? Thus far, Americans have opted for the cheap socks over and against American industry and national security.

Here's the bottom line, less money equals less buying power. Less buying power equals less freedom. Less freedom equals more government control. More government control equals the need for increased revenue. Increased revenue equals less money, and we start the cycle over again. How do we break out of this cycle? Well, we will never break the cycle until we break the bonds of greed, and it's unlikely that we will break the bonds of greed unless we structure our society around something more meaningful and more productive than the pursuit of happiness. Let the government decrease its revenue while our citizens increase their revenue and their sense of responsibility to family and community. Not only will this enable us to start breaking free from the economic tyranny that controls us, it will also enable us to find true happiness by fulfilling our responsibilities. A Reformation in Responsibility involves the restoration of American Industry and the understanding that people should keep the vast majority of their money in their pockets rather than in the government's coffers.

Questions for Reflection:
What is your initial reaction to this essay?

What did you agree/disagree with in this essay? Why?

Do you think increasing our debt to the degree that we have has helped or hurt our overall economic situation?

My summary of this essay:

Essay 8
Social Security & the Sanctity of Marriage

Genesis 2:24 – Therefore a man shall leave his father and mother and be joined to his wife, and they shall become one flesh. (NKJV)

The homosexual community will never destroy the sanctity of marriage. No doubt, some readers are wondering why I would say such a thing. The reason is simple; the heterosexual community beat them to it by destroying the sanctity of marriage before the LGBT agenda even got started. Yet, the importance of marriage for any society remains unchanged. The intertwining of a man's life and a woman's life is the double helix of society, and that truth will never change, no matter how much we tamper with it. When marriage is undertaken with a sense of responsibility toward one's family and society, it gives direction to a family, to a community, and to a nation. Strong marriages are like a budget surplus to a nation. They provide strength and stability. Unfortunately, our nation hasn't pursued either for some time now. It's sad that our nation's elected leaders can't seem to put a balanced budget on the table, but they're quick to promote same-sex marriage and the repeal of Don't Ask Don't Tell, moving both the American economy and the American family in the same failed direction.

The sanctity of marriage has been absent from our nation for quite some time. In large part, this is due to the weakness of the Church. It's hypocritical for Christians to take a strong stand against homosexuality while at the same time turning a blind eye to the dysfunctional and irresponsible activity of heterosexuals. As a minister, I'm confronted with heterosexual sin on a regular basis. The general sentiment that people are entitled to pursue their own happiness, regardless of the negative effects it will have on the lives of those around them, is to blame for much of the domestic dysfunction in our country. This irresponsible pursuit of happiness is a cultural epidemic. Fornication, co-habitation, infidelity, and divorce are rampant in our society because they are all rooted in the same thing, self-centered irresponsibility. The discipline and sense of responsibility needed to refrain from living together before establishing that which a legal marriage represents (e.g. joint property ownership, a plan for wealth distribution in the event of death, etc.) is the same discipline needed to keep a marriage together when things get tough, and all marriages have their tough times. Why is there such a lack of discipline and responsibility in our society? You guessed it—it's due to irresponsible individualism and the ignoble pursuit of happiness at all costs. When I counsel couples, and I have counseled hundreds over the years, it's pretty clear that one thing usually drives the relationship, the pursuit of happiness, and when the happiness ends so does the relationship.

Social security doesn't come in the form of a government check. If you want social security, then make people, not the government, responsible for taking care of one another.

Our society has forgotten that marriage is a sacred responsibility precisely because marriage is much more than two people making a decision to live "happily ever after." With no exaggeration, the success or failure of a marriage has an enormous impact on the rest of society. Ask any District Attorney in the country to identify the biggest drain on the U.S. court system, and many of them will cite domestic issues resulting from failed relationships and unfulfilled responsibilities as the major drain on the U.S. court system. Domestic dysfunction drains our economy as men and women pay lawyers millions of dollars that should be going toward the benefit and stability of their families and futures. Fractured families drain our workforce as the stresses and strains of failed relationships distract people from their daily work and force them to appear before judges during the week. Imagine the number of lost hours in the labor force over the course of a generation. Most importantly, broken homes drain our children socially and emotionally as they bounce back and forth from one parent to another. Yet, secular and liberal leaders naively think the best way forward is establishing the individual's right to same sex marriage and eventually polygamous marriage. If the courts think they're burdened with the domestic dysfunction of people who try to do marriage the traditional way, they had better "buckle their judicial seat belts" for the roller coaster of dysfunction that will come in the decades ahead as those who want nothing to do with the traditions of the past start showing up for their hearings.

When it comes to the dysfunction of our society, the government is like a weak parent that doesn't have the ability to say no to an irresponsible child who is emotionally and financially draining the rest of the family. Case in point, when the government provides a living for a woman who has five children from five different men, none of whom provide any child support, then the government enables dysfunction and masks the superiority of responsible living. Refusing to provide assistance to irresponsible people is the best way to demonstrate the negative effects of irresponsible living. No doubt, some would say that's not a compassionate or Christian response, but from a biblical perspective, God has no problem letting irresponsible people suffer the negative consequences of their actions. Hell is the quintessential example of people being forced to take responsibility for their beliefs and actions—a point that will be discussed further in Essay 13. Propping up irresponsible and dysfunctional lifestyles actually encourages others to live irresponsibly and creates social insecurity. That's why the current welfare system in America is destined for failure. The more irresponsible our society becomes, the more the government becomes responsible for social irresponsibility. Thus, the only way to reform our society is to reform the current system. The government needs to stop enabling dysfunction and irresponsibility in order to force people to start taking responsibility for the well being of their family members.

You see, social security doesn't come in the form of a government check. If you want social security, then make people, not the government, responsible for taking care of one another. Authentic social security is found in the way a husband treats his wife. It is found in the way adult children treat their elderly parents. If your marriage is strong and you raise your kids to have a strong work ethic, to honor their elders, and to respect authority, then you will have social security—a social security that's infinitely better than a government check. Social security starts and ends with strong marriages and strong families. Although our selfishness has destroyed the sanctity of marriage, nothing will ever take away the importance of marriage. Marriage will always be the most important institution in society, and our nation will prove this one way or another. Either we will return to the traditional values that built this nation and the government will start promoting social responsibility, or we will continue to grow as a welfare state, and we will decline further into the abyss of irresponsibility. If America is to succeed in the future, the people of the United States need to stand against heterosexual irresponsibility, same-sex marriage, and polygamy, and they need to take a courageous stand for the defense of traditional marriage.

Questions for Reflection:
What is your initial reaction to this essay?

What did you agree/disagree with in this essay? Why?

What are your thoughts about same sex-marriage?

My summary of this essay:

Essay 9
Welfare Education

Proverbs 4:7 – Getting wisdom is the wisest thing you can do! And whatever else you do, develop good judgment.(NLT)

While working on a doctorate at Princeton Theological Seminary, I had a colleague who was an up and coming star in American evangelicalism. Admittedly, his readings in theology and his writing skills were not as strong as they needed to be for the environment, and in the end, he washed out of the program. Yet there was an irony to it all—he was the only member of the program who had published a book. He shared with me how the publishing opportunity came about. He was leading a unique worship experience that was drawing roughly 2,000 young adults every weekend. The event gained the attention of a prominent evangelical pastor, and eventually a mentor/mentee relationship developed between them. In short order, he received a call, no doubt influenced by that pastor, from one of the most influential publishing houses in Christianity. The publisher wanted to meet and discuss the possibilities of a book. Somewhat surprised, my former colleague said something to the effect of, "I don't have any book ideas in mind." "That's alright," the editor replied. "We have a couple of ideas for you." To that he said, "I don't really write that well." "Don't worry," the editor said, "we'll pair you up with a team that will help you with the writing." My colleague was no fool, and he recognized straight away what was happening. The fact that the publisher's primary concern was money, not the book, is a reflection of the problem with education in America, of which the writing of books is a large part. Education, be it formal or informal, should not be about money. The essence of education is lost if education is pursued as a means to more money. Likewise, public education is destined to fail when administrators make decisions based on money (e.g. the amount of money a school system can get from the government or the amount of money lost from lawsuits filed by disgruntled students and/or parents).

Education is not a right. It was never a right and it will never be a right. Education is a privilege that demands discipline and responsibility.

There is a threefold essence to a true formal education: First, a formal education can be a means to an end (i.e. college, a good job, money, etc.), but true education is an end in itself. Education should foster lifelong learning. Children should be educated in such a way that they enjoy learning about the world around them. Second, true education properly respects the individual. That is not to say that education falls into the trap of irresponsible individualism by failing to hold individual students, teachers, or administrators accountable for poor decisions. Rather, true education acknowledges the fact that children learn differently. Teachers teach differently. Administrators administrate differently. Thus, educational success for one student can look markedly different from educational success for another student. One teacher's classroom and curriculum may be very different from that of a colleague. A variety of administrators should reflect a variety of administrative styles. Thirdly, true education is about living. It's about applying learning to life. Thus, if education does not involve moral formation, which leads to responsible living, then education is reduced to its lowest level—the retention of facts and successful performance on standardized tests.

Public education has, like many areas of American society, moved in the direction of government over-involvement. This move has led to the development of a Department of Education that holds itself responsible for the education of America's children, but this is not the government's responsibility. It is the responsibility of parents, grandparents, guardians, and local communities to educate children. The government's over-involvement creates a number of issues. It leads to a centralization of power, an incredibly wasteful bureaucracy, and problematic policies like No Child Left Behind. In turn, these issues result in top-down policies that standardize education in such a way that little room is left for individual nuances among students, teachers, and administrators, thus violating a major tenet of education. Isn't it ironic that a government obsessed with individualism refuses to honor the constructive individualism that is an inherent part of an authentic educational experience. Furthermore, when the government redistributes wealth among public schools, it masks failures and successes. For instance, if the government backed away from dictating what public schools can and cannot do, then L.A. County Schools or San Francisco County Schools could do what they want with money and morality, and traditional communities in the South could make their own decisions with respect to their schools. In short order, the better way to live would play itself out before the entire nation, and the economic and moral bankruptcy of the two would serve as an example of what not to do. Conversely, the secular ridicule often directed at traditional values would come to an abrupt halt because the evidence of success and failure would be on clear display.

The irresponsible individualism that has created a welfare state within our nation's economy has also affected our nation's educational system. The policies that are coming down from the Department of Education are nothing short of welfare education. A classic example of this is the "no zero" policies adopted by some schools. In schools that adopt ZAP (Zeros aren't Permitted) policies, a child can refuse to turn in work and still receive a grade. The rationale for such a policy is to prevent a child from being overly discouraged in the process of education and to make sure no child slips so far behind that he/she is left behind. This type of thinking is a direct result of the misdirected No Child Left Behind Act. The combination of irresponsible individualism and welfare education has resulted in an environment where the courts feel compelled to champion the cause of every disgruntled family, administrators are fearful of being sued for doing the right thing, teachers are given less and less freedom to do their jobs and actually teach, and students feel they are entitled to pass because education, like the pursuit of happiness, is one of their rights. In a world where the government is responsible for providing an education because education is a right, the essence of education is lost, and the goal becomes getting everyone through the system. Here's a bitter truth—everyone involved in the public school system knows that getting through the system is not the same as getting an education. The system is broken.

Wake up call—education is not a right. It was never a right and it will never be a right. Education is a privilege that demands discipline and responsibility. If public education was decentralized and authority was returned to the local level, communities would have a greater sense of ownership in the process of education and the need for government funding would be significantly reduced. Furthermore, localizing education would restore moral formation to the process of education as communities, not the government, would take responsibility for the actions of their children. If the Department of Education is decentralized, there is no doubt that some school systems will fail and others will enjoy great success, but the successes and failures will provide excellent examples of what to do and what not to do. A Reformation in Responsibility demands that education be returned to the local level so that parents and communities can take responsibility for the education and moral formation of their children.

Questions for Reflection:
What is your initial reaction to this essay?

What did you agree/disagree with in this essay? Why?

Do you think the public school system in America is heading in the right direction? Explain your answer.

My summary of this essay:

Essay 10
STATE OF CONFUSION

Isaiah 5:20-21 – Woe to those who call evil good, and good evil; who put darkness for light, and light for darkness; Who put bitter for sweet, and sweet for bitter! Woe to those who are wise in their own eyes, and prudent in their own sight!(NKJV)

In general, the people of the United States are doing things that are exactly opposite what needs to be done in order for the nation to succeed. In the name of individual rights, activist judges violate the rights of the majority of our people. In the name of fair labor standards, government backed unions have forced American labor and industry overseas. In the name of compassion, we expand entitlement programs that encourage irresponsibility and further drain an already weak financial system. In the name of human rights, we compromise our social foundations (i.e. the traditional family) by discarding traditional values and encouraging the individual pursuit of happiness in whatever manner an individual defines happiness. In the name of social progress and social security, the people of the United States have given the government the responsibility for training our children and taking care of the elderly and the dying. In sum: the government, via the courts, makes decisions that overturn the democratic decisions of the majority of our people; the government dictates the minimum wages and benefits that American corporations must provide American citizens; the government assumes responsibility for people's irresponsibility; the government assumes the responsibility for redefining marriage under the guise of human rights; and the government assumes responsibility for children and the elderly. Where does all of this increased government responsibility lead us as a nation?

Understandably, the result of increased government responsibility is increased taxes or, as many politicians like to say, "increased revenue," but whose revenue is it? It's certainly not the people's revenue because the nation is sinking further into debt. To return to our question, where does increased government responsibility lead us as a nation? Answer: It leads us to ruin. We are literally witnessing the demise of our nation, but that should come as no surprise. What else should we expect when our nation sits in the eye of the perfect philosophical storm? Thus far, the damage from the storm is the general sentiment that: 1) we are the best society that has ever lived (evolutionary thought); 2) we are the smartest society that has ever lived (the exaltation of human reason and science); and 3) the individual pursuit of happiness should be the primary concern of our society (irresponsible individualism). Unless we change the general sentiment of our nation, the social dysfunction that we witness in our society today is only a precursor of greater dysfunction that will come tomorrow.

> *The next time you hear someone from the media, a professor, or a scientist attempt to depict something as normal when it is clearly abnormal, call it what it is—a pseudotype.*

Our confused way of thinking is depicted in our use of the term "stereotype." In our society, stereotypes are generally rejected on the basis that they are overly simplistic and uncritical. Yet, the etymology of "stereotype" comes from the

Greek *stereos* "solid" and *tupos* "type," literally a "solid type" which implies an accurate depiction or image of something. The term was originally used by the Greeks to refer to casting molds. Only during the 20th century do we see the term popularized as an uncritical and therefore inaccurate assessment of something. Ironically, our culture bristles at stereotypes, but it is more than willing to accept a "pseudotype." Let me explain. Most people would recognize the Greek term *pseudos* "false" or "fake," which is the basis for our prefix (pseudo). For purposes of this work, I'm using "pseudotype" to refer to falsely depicting something as typical when, in actuality, it is atypical. In other words, the next time you hear someone from the media, a professor, or a scientist attempt to depict something as normal when it is clearly abnormal, call it what it is—a pseudotype.

Here's an example, I recently read an educational article suggesting that parental involvement is not necessary for student success in school. That may be true in some cases, but those cases would be exceptions. Statistics have demonstrated time and again that parental involvement is the determining factor in long term student success. These researchers found a few cases that were exceptions to the rule and, in pseudotypical fashion, promote the atypical as if it's typical. Likewise, secularists will search the world four times over to find evidence of homosexuality in the animal world and find nothing substantial, but when they find two male penguins in a zoo in Toronto, Canada that spend an inordinate amount of time with one another, they'll proclaim that they have evidence to support homosexuality in the animal world. Paradoxically, our culture is quick to reject stereotypes, regardless of how accurate they may be, but even quicker to accept pseudotypes, regardless of how inaccurate they might be.

The pseudotypical thinking of liberals and secularists has dominated our civil philosophy for over half a century. Thus, it would be beneficial to discuss the outcomes of pseudotypical thought. As has already been discussed in previous essays, many liberals and secularists are quick to defend the minority opinion because they see it as an issue of justice and human rights. They are quick to reject common sense because they do not want to see themselves as common. Rather, they want to believe that they are more intelligent than the common person, which, as described above, is also why they eschew stereotypes. Lastly, they are quick to reject traditional values and principles because they believe the modern scientific era is beyond such passé rules and morals. In short, pseudotypical thinking has crippled the strongest nation in the world. The proof is in the historical record. The traditional values of our forefathers and foremothers (e.g. a common Christian ethic, strong families, strong industry, independence, responsibility, etc.) built our nation out of nothing, and in short order, our adolescent attitudes have resulted in the fracturing of the family, the loss of industry, blatant irresponsibility on the part of our people, an overdependence on the government, and a general state of confusion.

As dismal as this may seem, the people of the United States can work themselves out of this confusing dilemma. In order to turn things around, people need to see the cloud formations of the perfect philosophical storm as they come together in the words and actions of their leaders. Hallmarks of pseudotypical thinkers and leaders are: 1) rejecting the wisdom of the past; 2) promoting government responsibility over and against individual and community responsibility; 3) promoting the minority opinion over and against the majority opinion; 4) promoting math and science over the arts and humanities; 5) using the courts to force cultural changes that a true democratic process would not allow; 6) refusing to restore American industry; and 7) refusing to demand not only a balanced budget but also a budget surplus. Undoubtedly, not all liberals and secularists will reflect each of these hallmarks in their thinking, but leaders who reflect all of these hallmarks should be replaced as soon as possible as they are a major hindrance to the future success of our nation. A Reformation in Responsibility demands that people replace pseudotypical leaders with leaders that will: 1) value the wisdom found in traditional values and morals; 2) seek to limit the role of the federal government and shift responsibilities to the state, local, and individual level; 3) value majority rights; 4) value the humanities as much as math and science; 5) only use the courts to enforce, not create, laws; 6) restore American industry; and 7) demand a budget surplus.

There is very little middle ground on the direction our society needs to pursue. In our current state of confusion, we have become the pseudotypical generation described by the prophet Isaiah that calls bitter sweet and sweet bitter; where dark is light and light is dark; where evil is tolerated as good and good is considered an intolerant evil. A large portion of the blame for our current state of confusion rests on the shoulders of a silent Church whose theology reflects Enlightenment philosophy more than it reflects biblical theology. Just as the Protestant Reformation served as a precursor to the Enlightenment, a reformation in the theology of the 21st century Church is a necessary antecedent to a Reformation in Responsibility that affects the larger society. In essence, the 21st century Church must be willing to abandon theological individualism, which is the topic of the next chapter, and return to biblical theology.

Questions for Reflection:
What is your initial reaction to this essay?

What did you agree/disagree with in this essay? Why?

Give a recent example of pseudotypical thinking that you witnessed either in the news, at work, at school, talking with friends, or in some other setting.

My summary of this essay:

Chapter 3

Theological Individualism

Like the rise of secular individualism, theological individualism has developed over the course of centuries, and it follows a logical path. This chapter will focus on three stages in the development of theological individualism, namely, the Protestant Reformation, 19th century American revivalism, and the rise of American evangelicalism. Each of these stages has contributed to the modern crisis in America. A large part of the problem is the fact that American Christianity is influenced more by post-Enlightenment philosophy and modern individualism than by biblical theology. For all practical purposes, much of Western Christianity has pursued the happiness of humanity more than it has pursued the holiness of God. The only difference between the general message of the Church and the message of secular philosophy is the focal point. The focal point for secular philosophy is a person's security and happiness in this life. The focal point for modern Christian theology is the individual's security and happiness in the afterlife. Despite the difference in context, this life or the afterlife, the individual's happiness rather than the individual's service and responsibility to God and humanity has been the essential concern for Western philosophy and theology.

If things are going to change, our focal point needs to change. The message of the State needs to change from emphasizing society's service to the individual to emphasizing the individual's service to society. Likewise, the message of the Church needs to change from one that focuses on God's service to humanity to one that stresses humanity's service to God. Don't misunderstand what is being said here. It would be inappropriate for the Church to dismiss the concept of God's service to humanity. Undoubtedly, God's service to humanity through the work of the Christ is an overarching theme in Christian theology, but it's only part of the Christian message. Another overarching theme of biblical theology is the fact that we were created to worship and serve God, not on our terms but on God's terms. The greatest commandment in Scripture is to love the Lord with all your heart, soul, and strength (Deuteronomy 6:5; Mark 12:30). The second command is to love your neighbor as yourself (Leviticus 19:18; Mark 12:31). The theological individualism of our day reverses the two, and teaches that the most important commandment is to love our neighbors as we would love ourselves, which means that we should allow our neighbors to do whatever they would like to do in their pursuit of happiness. Such thinking violates both commands because it places individual desires before divine holiness, and it places the individual pursuit of happiness before the needs of one's family and the larger society.

For all practical purposes, much of Western Christianity has pursued the happiness of humanity more than it has pursued the holiness of God.

A return to the essential teachings of Scripture is the only way the theological table will be turned right side up. Likewise, a return to biblical principles and holiness in the Church will help our larger society turn away from its unbalanced pursuit of happiness. The beauty of biblical theology is that it is a self-correcting system that has the potential to bring balance to an individual, a family, a denomination, or a nation. Where there is bitterness, the Bible leads to forgiveness. Where there is tolerance for sin, the Bible leads to condemnation. Where there is self-righteousness, the Bible leads to humility. Where there is a disregard for people who are hurting around us, the Bible leads to grace and compassion. Where there is a lack of emphasis on the holiness of God, the Bible leads us to the fear of the Lord, which is the beginning of wisdom. In the decades to come, Christian congregations and denominations must rise above the rituals, polity, and theological nuances that have long divided them, and they must stand together on the biblical principles that unite them. Western Christianity must address the irresponsible individualism of our day by first addressing the unbiblical theological individualism that it has been promoting from its pulpits. In short, if the Church has the courage to correct itself, then it has the ability to initiate another reformation—a Reformation in Responsibility.

Essay 11
The Protestant Reformation & Pandora's Box

Proverbs 22:28 – Do not remove the ancient landmark that your ancestors set up. (NRSV)

The theological shifts that took place during the Protestant Reformation were necessary changes for the sixteenth century Church, but as a former professor of mine often said, "The Protestant Reformation was about some things. It wasn't about everything." That is a point that the 21st century Church needs to remember. Some of the more recognized concerns of the Reformation, such as the individual's right to interpret the Bible as the sole rule of faith (*sola scriptura*) and the ability for the individual to receive justification by faith alone (*sola fide*), were legitimate issues, but in large part they were a reflection of the underlying issue of the day—the relationship between the institution and the individual. The fact that the reformers frequently appealed to the Church Fathers in order to justify their theological positions was proof that *sola scriptura* was a noble but unrealistic goal, insomuch as, the Bible may be the primary source of divine revelation for Christians, but it is not the only source Christians use to understand divine revelation. Every Christian community uses pastors, teachers, trusted commentaries, and other theological sources in order to better understand the Bible. Although those sources are not venerated like the Bible, and rightfully so, the Bible is not used without them. Likewise, *sola fide* sounds appealing, but it did not take the reformers long to set up their own ecclesial hoops, via denominational catechisms, for people to jump through. Thus, critiques of the Protestant Reformation often deal with the surface issues more than the core issue of the relationship between the individual and the institution. Furthermore, it is a mistake to think that famous reformers like Luther and Calvin initiated the challenge to the Pope. Rather, they highlighted and moved forward the already existing tensions of their era. Indeed, the Protestant Reformation was the inevitable result of growing tensions between the role of the individual/local congregation, which had little influence, and the role of the most influential institution in Europe, the Church. In a similar manner, the challenge of our day is to address the growing tension between the role of the majority/Christian Church, which now has little influence in society, and the role of the most influential institution in the West, namely, the secular courts.

To return to the reformers, their challenge to the church was not entered into lightly, and even Luther was convinced that he was not leaving the Church as much as he was seeking to reform it. However, Johann von Staupitz, Luther's mentor, expressed great concern that the Reformation would open the proverbial Pandora's Box and destroy the unity of the Church. Staupitz was spot on in his estimation of the long term implications of the Reformation. For as much good as the Reformation accomplished, it also put in motion an untold number of denominational splits and heresies. Sadly, many contemporary Christian denominations no longer follow biblical theology precisely because their sense of independence encourages them to rely on their own conclusions rather than relying on the authority of the Church at large. With respect to theological matters, it is often said that Christians should "major on

> *On matters where the Church has spoken with one voice throughout the ages (e.g. the reality of heaven and hell, the Lordship of Christ, the understanding of marriage, etc.), it is the responsibility of the contemporary Church to continue speaking with that voice.*

the majors and minor on the minors." That sounds like good advice, but the problem is that people can't agree on what's a major and what's a minor. When there is a disagreement on matters of faith and practice, the historic teachings of the Church should assist us in determining the proper course of action for the future. On matters where the Church has spoken with one voice throughout the ages (e.g. the reality of heaven and hell, the Lordship of Christ, the understanding of marriage, etc.), it is the responsibility of the contemporary Church to continue speaking with that voice. Thus, contrary to secular opinion and liberal theology, there is a general consensus among virtually all Christian communities of all eras on certain matters of the Christian faith.

Of course, some academics will be quick to say there has been little consensus, as evidenced by the "lost Christianities" of the Early Church Period, but that's a classic example of pseudotypical theology. Liberal scholarship will consistently argue that a spurious Gnostic text, that was unknown prior to the 20th century, should be considered as important to the understanding of Christianity as the four canonical gospels. That should come as no surprise in an era when some argue that same-sex marriage is considered as important to society as traditional marriage even though the former has no historical precedent. The notion that Christianity is a diverse belief system that provides a smorgasbord of theological options from which to choose is a recent notion that is not historically accurate or biblically sound. Rather, the notion is a reflection of modern academic bias and modern theological individualism. Liberal theological scholarship, like liberal secularism, asserts that the individual/minority opinion takes precedence over the historical teachings of the Church on matters of faith and biblical interpretation. However, it makes little sense that an individual, even if he/she has the perceived credibility that comes with ordination or an advanced theological degree, should have the right to dismiss the major tenets of Christianity and still call himself/herself a Christian. Yet, due to the combination of philosophical and theological individualism that pervades our society, that is precisely what we have allowed.

The Episcopal Church is an example of this dilemma. When a denomination in America decides it will support homosexuality in the ranks of its clergy despite the historical teachings of the Church at large, it reflects the typical self-centered irresponsible individualism that expects God, society, and thousands of years of tradition to bow before the sentiments of a few who want to do it their own way. If homosexuality was commensurate with Christianity, then it would have been embraced during the first century of the Common Era when homosexuality, bisexuality, and promiscuous heterosexual behavior were commonplace in the Roman Empire. Christianity rejected all of those practices. On what grounds are modern Christians expected to reverse the teachings of the Church with respect to sexuality? On the grounds that society has progressed? How can the modern acceptance of homosexuality, bisexuality, and heterosexual promiscuity be an example of positive sociological evolution when Western civilization once practiced those things with regularity and then determined, from the Byzantine Period to the 20th century, that those practices were publically unacceptable and socially destructive? Our irresponsible heterosexual activity and the promotion of same-sex marriage is not a progression in evolutionary psychology. Rather, it is a digression in basic morality. At least the ancient Greeks and Romans relegated their sexual exploits to the realm of pleasure and refused to establish families and communities around homosexual and bisexual relationships.

Despite the sentiments of some contemporary Christian groups, the Protestant Reformation, with all of its positive and negative consequences, is over. A new reformation is necessary for the Church of the 21st century. In a world of destructive diversity and irresponsible individualism, the challenge for the Church is unity and responsibility. We must find a way to unite orthodox congregations of all Christian denominations in order to stand together and influence our society for good. For the last few centuries, our allegiance has been to individual happiness, then to our society and government, and lastly to whatever gods a person wants to serve, but that is wrong. Our first responsibility is to God, who alone is the simultaneous embodiment of grace and truth. Our second responsibility is to our local community—starting with our families. Then, when we fulfill these first two responsibilities, we are prepared to be responsible to our government by holding our government accountable to the best interests of society at large. Lastly, when these responsibilities are fulfilled, then we are free to pursue happiness, however we may define it, because we will have already defined happiness within the parameters of social responsibility. A Reformation in Responsibility demands that the 21st century Church reorder its sense of responsibility.

Questions for Reflection:
What is your initial reaction to this essay?

What did you agree/disagree with in this essay? Why?

How does Proverbs 22:28 relate to this essay?

My summary of this essay:

Essay 12
INDIVIDUALISM & AMERICAN REVIVALISM

Psalm 144:3 – LORD, what is a human, that You take knowledge of him? Or the son of man, that You are mindful of him?(NKJV)

In order to understand the importance of the individual in American Christianity, one need not look any further than the revivalism of the Great Awakening (mid-1700's) and the Second Great Awakening (early 1800's). The Awakenings had a major impact on the minds and hearts of Americans during the eighteenth and nineteenth centuries, and they helped set the course for the future of American religion. This is important to understand because another awakening is possible and, in many ways, is an absolute necessity for the future success of America. Secondly, it is important to understand that revival services were the essential events of the Awakenings as they sought to "revive" people in their commitments to God—commitments that were represented in a "decision for Christ." Thus, to recap, the essential event of the Awakenings was the revival. The primary purpose of a revival was a decision for Christ, and the core concern in a decision for Christ was the individual's relationship with God. For those unfamiliar with the evangelical tradition, the expression "decision for Christ," is used to refer to an individual's decision to accept God's offer of salvation through Christ by confessing and repenting of one's sins and determining to live a new life of faith in service to God.

Over time, the legitimate concern for the individual's salvation, which is embodied in the "decision for Christ" event, overwhelmed the concern for the individual's commitment to serve God. By the middle of the 20th century, the near solitary concern of American evangelicalism had become the individual's salvation. By the end of the 20th century, American evangelicalism would be so preoccupied with the security and happiness of the individual that the theological table would be completely turned upside down and the dominant message sounding forth from American pulpits was an overemphasis on God's service to humanity with very little attention, if any, being given to the individual's submission to God. Such theological individualism is epitomized by a popular saying among evangelical ministers and revival preachers, namely, "If you were the only sinner on the earth, Christ would die for you!" Really—where is that in the Bible?

With relative ease, one can piece together various biblical passages in order to argue that God loves the individual (the fact that God knows the number of hairs on your head, the fact that Christ is willing to leave the 99 sheep in order to find one lamb that is lost, the fact that Christ came to serve not to be served, etc.). Yet, if you were the only spiritual failure on the planet and everyone else was doing a decent job of serving God, should God die for you? Is one misdirected human life that important? Our civil philosophy and theology answer that question with a resounding, "Yes!" We want to believe we are that important, but that is a major part of our problem. We are not that important. You are not that important. I am not that important. Creation itself cries out that God did not create us with that level of importance. Our planet could implode, and the natural order of our neighboring galaxy would not even be affected. God does not need us. The universe does not need us. The earth does not need us. Considering the degree to which we have destroyed our planet in the last century, the earth would be better off without us. The narcissistic notion that God is sitting in the heavens with nothing else to do but watch over the earth and wring His hands over our bad decisions is a completely inaccurate depiction of the majesty and mystery of the One who sits in the heavens and laughs at those who rebel against Him (Psalm 2).

This unbalanced theology, with respect to the role of the individual, is why our society's sense of justice is so skewed. It's hard to argue, from a judicial perspective, that the majority opinion does not need to bend over backwards to accommodate the minority opinion when at the same time you're arguing, from a theological perspective, that the God of all creation should be willing to die for one misdirected human being. This type of philosophy and theology is why our penal system protects the rights of serial killers and pedophiles. In our skewed system, it doesn't matter what the individual does or how much innocence the individual destroys; God and society should still love the individual because individuals are supposed to be loved regardless of what they do—full stop. That's how important individuals are in God's eyes, right? Actually, from a biblical perspective, that's wrong. Individuals aren't that important in God's economy—that's why the majority of them are damned (Matt. 7:13-14). Of course, some readers will be incensed at this idea because this type of thinking is directly opposed to the theological individualism of our era that, without publicly articulating it, has actually made one human life more important than God.

> *The heart of Christianity is not the salvation of the individual. The heart of Christianity is the worship of the Living God.*

The Shack is a classic portrayal of modern theological individualism. William Paul Young is an excellent writer and the book is a great read, but it was somewhat confusing that so many people said the book challenged modern notions of God. Sure, picturing God the Father as Aunt Jemima making pancakes in the morning will challenge the imagination of most Christians, but the challenge is superficial. God transcends race and gender. However, when it came to the essence and nature of God, the real stuff of theology, *The Shack* was completely in step with modern irresponsible individualism. The book presented a God who looks at a sadistic and presumably unrepentant child killer with mercy and compassion and expects His followers to do the same. As popular as that message was, it's completely out of step with the message of Christ. When Jesus taught about children, he didn't say, "Whoever harms one of these little one's will be OK because it all works out in the end." Rather, he said of those who harm children, "It would be better for him if a millstone was hung around his neck and he was thrown into the sea." Here's an important question; "For those who harm children, being drowned is better than what?" Answer—it's better than God getting His divine hands on them and destroying their souls. That's how Jesus looks at it. You see, there are long term implications for a society that does not have the courage and conviction to protect its children by punishing pedophiles and child killers. Such a society punishes itself with its lack of justice.

The notion that every individual has inherent worth regardless of the way one lives his/her life is a comical fiction from both a theological and a secular perspective. First, from the perspective of Christian theology, such a notion is depicted in another popular saying among evangelicals, namely, "God loves Hitler as much as He loves Mother Teresa." Such theology robs the latter of the commendation of a virtuous life and it absolves the former of being responsible for blatant evils that demand divine judgment. If God loves everyone the same way, then why does Psalm 5:4-5 say, "For You are not a God who takes pleasure in wickedness, nor shall evil dwell with You. The boastful shall not stand in Your sight; You hate all workers of iniquity?"(NKJV) Not only is theological individualism unbiblical, it also lacks rationality and respectability in the minds of non-Christians. Second, from a secular perspective, it is somewhat of an oxymoron to argue that every individual has worth and value. If God does not exist and there is no such thing as eternity, then our lives have no lasting value. That is not to say that we cannot make a positive contribution to the world, but it is obvious that our contributions, in the absence of eternity, have no lasting significance. With such a worldview, what is the lasting purpose of life? With such a worldview, the life of a human is no different than the life of a plant. Of course, that's what the Bible has been teaching for thousands of years. Psalm 103:15-16 describes life apart from eternity, "Our days on earth are like grass; like wildflowers, we bloom and die. The wind blows, and we are gone-- as though we had never been here."(NLT) Ultimately, our worth and value is found in the fact that we have been created for a purpose, and that purpose is the glory of God. When a person abandons God, he/she simultaneously abandons the purpose for which he/she was created.

Another religious awakening is essential for reversing our irresponsible individualism. A national revival is the only thing that will change the narcissistic attitudes and actions of our people. Yet, recasting the old-time-religion revivals of the 1800's will not work. The very essence of a new revival needs to be markedly different from the revivals of the past. The fact that God does not insure that the majority of individuals will be saved is proof that the individual is not God's primary concern. We need to be awakened to the fact that ultimately we were created to serve God not be served by God. Let's turn the theological table right side up by recognizing that the heart of Christianity is not the salvation of the individual. The heart of Christianity is the worship of the Living God. The individual is not the most important thing in life. The glory of God is the most important thing in life. The individual is not the centerpiece of Christian theology. God is the centerpiece of Christian theology—the Living God whose compassion provides salvation and whose justice demands damnation.

Questions for Reflection:
What is your initial reaction to this essay?

What did you agree/disagree with in this essay? Why?

Look up Matthew 7:13-14 and share your thoughts on the passage.

My summary of this essay:

Essay 13
Welfare Theology & the Problem of Hell

Proverbs 15:11 – Hell and Destruction are before the LORD; so how much more the hearts of the sons of men. (NKJV)

One of the greatest hindrances to the growth of Christianity in the West is welfare theology, that is, a theology in which God is responsible for every aspect of Christian growth and salvation while little, if any, responsibility is placed on the individual. There is no doubt that, from a biblical perspective, salvation is a work of God, a point that we will return to in a moment, but to say that God is responsible for every aspect of salvation is theologically irresponsible because it dismisses human responsibility. There is no way God can be responsible for every aspect of the process of salvation and at the same time be absolved of responsibility for the process of damnation. Many in the Reformed tradition would argue that all are damned and God has graciously made the decision to save some, but such an argument does not take into account that deciding to save some is by default a decision not to save others. So, we are presented with a dilemma. How can salvation be a gift from God while damnation is the result of human action, or in some cases, human inaction?

The idea that one must safeguard God's role in the process of salvation is absurd to say the least. Everything, even our existence, is a gift from God. The potential exists that, if God had willed it, we would not exist. God has given us life. Absolutely everything from the ability to breathe, live, love, laugh, etc. to the spiritual mysteries of salvation and sanctification are all gifts from God. Yet, God has ordered the world in such a way that what we do with those gifts is a matter of free will. When we wake up in the morning, God has given us a day to exercise our talents under the direction of our desires. Yet, we were not guaranteed that day. That day was a gift from God. Salvation is much the same. God offers us the gift of salvation in Christ. What we do with that gift is up to us, but the presentation of the gift was never up to us. Presenting the gift of salvation to the world was always God's choice and God's work. Thus, human freewill and effort will never threaten God's sovereignty and grace. No matter how hard a person may work at living a life that is pleasing to God, salvation, much like life itself, is never ours for the taking. Eternal life and mundane life are always God's generous gifts.

> *The concept of hell is a complete offense to our modern sensibilities because it's the quintessential example of people being held accountable for their actions.*

In our welfare culture, the biblical concept of "gift" needs to be qualified. In Romans 5-6, the Apostle Paul indicates that, salvation is a "free gift" in the sense that there is nothing we could do to demand it from God, but it is a gift with strings attached. Those who decide to accept the gift are obligated to use it, that is, to give themselves to God and to see their lives as "instruments of righteousness." (Romans 6:13) Understanding this is the point of departure between a welfare theology that places no responsibility on the individual and a theology of responsibility that holds the individual accountable for his/her relationship with God and, in turn, his/her relationship with the rest of society. However, the last thing secularists want to do is hold people accountable for their actions. Secularists have to find reasons to excuse the serial killer and the pedophile and the terrorist because if they don't, then their philosophical system collapses. If we can't excuse human violence and failure, then we have to admit that, despite evolution, despite all the attention we have given to the individual, and despite all our advancements in technology and science, we are no better than those who have gone before us, and in some cases we are worse. I recently listened to an interview on NPR where the interviewee preferred using the term "low empathy" rather than the term "evil" when describing murderers. He went on to explain that, among pathological killers, his research revealed abnormal behavior in the part of the brain that causes empathy. Do we really need a lengthy research project to determine that the mental activity of serial killers is something other than normal? A five year old child could tell us that. Call it "evil" or call it "low empathy," either way the person should be held accountable for his/her actions, but we are unwilling to do this in our day and age. Our culture is eager to excuse the serial killer or the pedophile because excusing the worst behavior among us is, in a roundabout way, an excuse for our own behavior.

The concept of hell is a complete offense to our modern sensibilities because it's the quintessential example of people being held accountable for their actions. Salvation is a gift, but it is not a right. Salvation demands responsibility. The concept of universal salvation/reconciliation is more a reflection of post-Enlightenment philosophy than a reflection of Christian theology. In 2003, while attending a seminar at Duke University on Luther and the Reformation in Germany, one of the Ph.D. candidates in the group shared her disdain for Luther's dogmatism. In particular, she completely rejected the idea of hell. The professor, in a non-threatening manner, simply said, "Well, Luther didn't come up with the idea of hell himself. There are people who believed it before him, like Augustine." "I don't care for Augustine either," she quipped back. "Well," he said, "It [the concept of hell] is in the B-I-B-L-E." That statement prompted a moment of laughter shared by everyone who grew up in a church setting singing the B-I-B-L-E song. After the laughter subsided, she responded with the typically modern approach to biblical studies, "Just because it's in the Bible doesn't mean it's true." What our professor said next surprised most of us. He paused for a moment and said, "It's your choice if you don't want to believe in hell, but you may want to pick another religion because with Christianity hell is part of the package." What our professor was getting at was more than a commitment to Christian dogma. He was addressing the theological dilemmas that occur when one tries to do away with hell.

Dismissing the concept of hell is to dismiss people of their responsibility and accountability to the world around them. Subsequently, such a move would be a dismissal of justice. There is no justice where people are not held accountable for their actions. Biblical theology emphasizes justice as much as it emphasizes grace. The challenge for Christian theology is finding the perfect point of tension that holds the two in balance. In closing this essay, the 21st century Church must stand against the popular and immature theology that wants salvation without sanctification, heaven without hell, and God without Satan—such theology presents a façade of academic sophistication, but in reality it is developed in order to accommodate the childish sensitivities of a society that does not want to deal with the harsh realities of life—hard work (the process sanctification), personal responsibility (the reality of hell), or evil (the personality of Satan). Part of a

Reformation in Responsibility involves recapturing the biblical concept of hell precisely because such a move restores justice by making the individual accountable to God and responsible to the world around him/her.

Questions for Reflection:
What is your initial reaction to this essay?

What did you agree/disagree with in this essay? Why?

Do you believe in hell? Why or why not?

My summary of this essay:

Essay 14
Failing to Succeed

Proverbs 9:12 — If you become wise, you will be the one to benefit. If you scorn wisdom, you will be the one to suffer. (NLT)

One of the major changes needed in our society is related to our willingness to allow people to fail and consequently experience the negative repercussions of their actions. However, like the concept of hell, letting people fail goes against our civil philosophy. For one thing, failure significantly hinders the pursuit of happiness, which is unacceptable to our modern psyche. In Essay 9, we discussed the ZAP (Zeros Aren't Permitted) policies that are promoted in many public school systems, which essentially amount to an educational bailout program at the individual level. Students can refuse to turn in work, and they will still get credit. Yet, this "failure isn't permitted" attitude permeates our entire society. Bankers make foolish decisions and lose billions of dollars, and the government bails them out. The government makes foolish decisions, and the taxpayers bail them out. People overextend themselves financially, and the system allows them to keep property that they did not pay for. Only in our misdirected culture do we consider people homeowners when they sign papers but make no payments. Newsflash—if you didn't pay for it, then you don't own it. All of these bailout programs exist because our culture believes that letting students fail or letting banks go under or shutting down wasteful government agencies or kicking people out of a house they never purchased will do irreparable harm to the larger society. Another newsflash—the harm has already been done. Life doesn't give passes for irresponsible behavior. In the end, irresponsible behavior will catch up with a person, a family, or a nation. In keeping with our examples, if we push children through a public education program but fail to truly educate them, then our nation will suffer because future generations do not have the education they need to move our society forward. With respect to the banking/debt crisis in Europe and America, it is irrational to expect that continued bailouts will work when: 1) the recipients are so irresponsible that they needed the bailout in the first place; and 2) the first series of bailouts have not turned the situation around. Lastly, a credit based society is a society destined for failure precisely because people are not assuming responsibility for property ownership and personal estate development which in turn provide for financial independence and security.

Life doesn't give passes for irresponsible behavior.

When people fail, their failure provides an illustration of what not to do. For example, if a woman lives irresponsibly and has four children by four different men who don't provide for her or the children, why should the rest of society be responsible for her unstable living conditions? When the government steps in and doles out welfare checks in order to prop up irresponsible and dysfunctional behavior, what is accomplished in the end? Once in a while someone breaks out of the cycle of irresponsibility and dysfunction, but the majority of time the end result is the same, namely, another family is put on the public dole. This may sound harsh, but from a Christian perspective, supporting that kind of irresponsibility is not supported in the Bible. The same Scriptures that tell us to have compassion on the poor and to take care of orphans and widows also says that we should not assume responsibility for people's blatant irresponsibility. 2 Thessalonians 3:6-11 states:

> But we command you, brethren, in the name of our Lord Jesus Christ, that you withdraw from every brother who walks disorderly and not according to the tradition which he received from us. For you yourselves know how you ought to follow us, for we were not disorderly among you; nor did we eat anyone's bread free of charge, but worked with labor and toil night and day, that we might not be a burden to any of you, not because we do not have authority, but to make ourselves an example of how you should follow us. For even when we were with you, we commanded you this: If anyone will not work, neither shall he eat. For we hear that there are some who walk among you in a disorderly manner, not working at all...(NKJV)

The Church should set an example of responsible hospitality by: 1) helping those who are trying their best but are struggling; and 2) allowing those who are blatantly irresponsible and lazy to fail.

People should be allowed to fail because failure serves as an example to the rest of society. The example that irresponsible behavior sets is a good one because intelligent people will decide not to follow it. Few things are more powerful than failure. Failure is one of life's greatest lessons. My grandfather used to say, "Learn from other people's mistakes. That way you don't have to make them." But that's hard to do when the government keeps hiding people's mistakes through entitlements programs and bailouts. Ironically, the Occupy Wall Street movement and the corporations that received bailouts have a common philosophical foundation, that is, both are willing to be dependent on the government. When the government props up dysfunctional individuals, banks, companies, etc., it only serves to encourage more dysfunction, and in the end it doesn't prop up anything. Rather, it knocks down the whole nation.

Secondly, people should be allowed to fail because their continued irresponsibility will drag down their family, the Church, and the society at large. Imagine a sports team that insisted on fielding a player who never showed up for practice, hardly ever worked out, and intentionally loused up the game because he didn't care about the goals and feelings of the rest of the team. That's unimaginable. Yet, that is exactly what we do when we try to keep irresponsible people on track with the rest of the society. Undoubtedly, someone will say, "Didn't God do just that by allowing dysfunctional human beings to crucify Christ on the cross?" Not really. When you look at the whole of biblical theology, God's character is never compromised by human dysfunction. Sure, Christ humbled Himself, took on human form, and died the death of the Cross (Philippians 2:5-8), but He did not remain there. After completing His atoning work, Christ rose from the grave, ascended to the heavens, and is now seated at the right hand of the Father. Make no mistake about it, God is not held captive by our failures. God allows us to make our own decisions. He allows people to fail. He even allows people to destroy themselves. Regardless of how corrupt humanity becomes, we will never corrupt the holiness of God. Yet, this is not the case with human relationships. People are easily influenced by the dysfunction and irresponsibility around them. Individuals that have no desire to work toward the good of society should be allowed to fail so that the society does not fail in its attempt to keep those individuals on par with the rest of the culture. Interestingly, God has

> *The greatest compliment you can give people is to hold them accountable to standards. Why would you hold people accountable to something if you did not believe they could do it?*

ordered humanity in this way. Individuals have one lifetime to cooperate with God's work in the world. Some people succeed at this and others fail. Regardless of individual success or failure, God demonstrates His willingness to clean the slate of humanity every hundred years and work with a completely new group.

Finally, people should be allowed to fail because failure forces a culture of responsibility and respect. Responsibility and respect go hand in hand. The greatest compliment you can give people is to hold them accountable to standards. Why would you hold people accountable to something if you did not believe they could do it? This brings us back to the concept of hell. Ironically, hell is as much about human potential as it is human failure. God created us with free will and great potential. God respects the potentiality of human beings. That's why God holds humans accountable for their actions. It would serve our society well to follow God's example and start creating a culture of responsibility and respect. We need to reform our culture by emphasizing the individual's responsibility to work toward the good of the larger society rather than emphasizing society's responsibility to accommodate the individual's desires. In short, we are failing to succeed as a society because our society doesn't believe that failing is part of succeeding. A Reformation in Responsibility will challenge us to embrace failure in order to succeed.

Questions for Reflection:

What is your initial reaction to this essay?

What did you agree/disagree with in this essay? Why?

How do you feel about letting people fail?

My summary of this essay:

Essay 15
Agnostic Preachers & Empty Pews

2 Timothy 4:3-4 – For the time is coming when people will not put up with sound doctrine, but having itching ears, they will accumulate for themselves teachers to suit their own desires, and will turn away from listening to the truth…(NRSV)

In contemporary biblical studies, vague is vogue. While completing three graduate programs of theology, I had countless conversations with people who were professing Christians, and in some cases were clergy, even though they had abandoned some of the major tenets of Christianity. The result of our politically correct vagueness is a paradox in the pulpit. In many churches in Europe and America the clergy standing behind the pulpits are not Christians. They are agnostics. Such is the case with many of the mainline denominations. I recall being at a seminar on contemporary Christianity at Princeton Theological Seminary when one of the professors from the Presbyterian Church (U.S.A.) said, "Of our churches that are declining the slowest—and I said that intentionally—for all practical purpose hardly any of them are growing…" As he went on with his lecture, I thought of many conversations I've had with mainline denominational leaders who insist that their churches are shrinking because the masses have sold out to ignorant fundamentalists who tickle their ears with words they want to hear. In reality, the preachers of liberal theology are the ones tickling people's ears by embracing the theological individualism of our day and abandoning the exclusive lordship of Jesus Christ, the inspiration of the Bible, the power of the Holy Spirit, and the reality of hell. It should be no surprise that much of Christianity is in decline. Many churches have left the faith. Thus, people are leaving the pews. If churches will restore biblical preaching to the pulpit, people will return to the pews.

Truth be known, much of intellectualism is perception. That is why one era's philosopher is another era's fool. The respected and tenured professors of our era who promote the vague theological individualism of our day would not be allowed to sweep the floor of a university during the late Medieval Period, a time when surety was the mark of the sage. Yet, make no mistake about it; surety is not completely absent from contemporary theology. In her book, *Beyond Belief: the Secret Gospel of Thomas*, Princeton University professor Elaine Pagels shares her perspective on the surety that modern research has attained with respect to the study of early Christianity:

One era's philosopher is another era's fool.

> Thanks to research undertaken since that time [since her 1979 publication *The Gnostic Gospels*] and shared by many scholars throughout the world, what that book [*The Gnostic Gospels*] attempted to offer as a kind of rough, charcoal sketch of the history of Christianity now can be seen as if under an electron microscope— yielding considerably more clarity, detail, and accuracy (p. 33).

Really, "under an electron microscope?" It's amazing that Pagels expects the reader to trust a modern scholarly assessment of early Christianity over and against the traditional teachings of the Church. You see, in the case of modern biblical scholarship, surety is applied to contemporary theological theories, but skepticism is applied to traditional theology. The same adolescent attitude reflected in the larger culture with respect to traditional values is apparent in biblical studies—reject the tradition, trust the new edition.

Most disturbing about the current trends in modern biblical studies is the blatant self-promotion that is accepted among scholars. For example, it's perfectly acceptable among intellectuals to allow one's bias to overtly influence scholarly studies if one happens to be a feminist, a homosexual, or generally from any group that intellectuals perceive as being marginalized by the rest of society. However, if your bias is connected to traditional values or the majority sentiment, you are quickly dismissed as one who lacks objectivity. This expression of theological individualism mimics the secular irresponsible individualism that we witness when activist judges hold the majority sentiment at bay while encouraging the minority sentiment to run its course freely. In the case of Professor Pagels, she states that her research enabled her to identify what she disliked about traditional Christianity, namely, "the tendency to identify Christianity with a single, authorized set of beliefs... coupled with the conviction that Christian belief alone offers access to God" (p. 29). No doubt her book encourages people to move beyond the beliefs of orthodox Christian doctrine, but what is truly "beyond belief" is the fact that Pagels' personal bias so clearly influences her research, yet her work is touted as an example of unbiased scholarship.

Only in our age of irresponsible individualism does a person have the ability to rewrite the rules and expect the larger group or society to make the necessary accommodations. As was mentioned in Essay 13, we want salvation, but we want to ignore the Savior. We want heaven, but we want to ignore the reality of hell. We want to join a tradition, but we want to ignore the traditional rules. We want to be a part of a faith community, but we want to ignore that community's faith. In a very real way, the influence of individualism is so pervasive in our society that the typical attitude of many churchgoers is, "If it matters to me, then it matters to God." That is why so many denominations are crippled in their ability to reach the world. The world looks right past our religious rhetoric and sees that modern Christianity is rather pathetic in its attempt to peddle the very thing that has already left the larger culture bankrupt, namely, the individual's irresponsible pursuit of happiness.

> *Only in our age of irresponsible individualism does a person have the ability to rewrite the rules and expect the larger group or society to make the necessary accommodations.*

There are many things that the Church does as part of its mission that other organizations can do just as well or even better (e.g. self-help programs, humanitarian service, medical assistance, etc.), but there is one thing that only the Church can do—worship the Living God in spirit and truth. Above all else, the Church should be promoting the glory of God. When churches abandon the moral and theological traditions of Christianity, they diminish their unique purpose in the world and forfeit their influence on society. Imagine buying tickets for a professional football game, and when you arrived at the stadium, no one played football. Rather, the team sat around talking and joking with one another—oblivious of the fans. Now, if this happened on a regular basis, how long should we expect that team to draw people to their stadium? Likewise, congregations that do not have the courage to proclaim the traditional teachings of Christianity should expect to lose members because, like football players that never play football, they have abandoned the task to which they were called. Part of a Reformation in Responsibility involves replacing agnostic preachers with ministers who are committed to orthodox Christianity.

Questions for Reflection:
What is your initial reaction to this essay?

What did you agree/disagree with in this essay? Why?

Describe ways that you have seen ministers and congregations abandon major aspects of Christian doctrine? What impact has this had on their denomination and/or congregation?

My summary of this essay:

Chapter Four

The Church In The 21st Century

The overarching purpose of the Church never changes. Jesus' words in Matthew 28:19-20, often referred to as the Great Commission, embody the mission of the church. "Go therefore and make disciples of all the nations, baptizing them in the name of the Father and of the Son and of the Holy Spirit, teaching them to observe all things that I commanded you; and lo, I am with you always, even to the end of the age."(NAS) Clearly, the mission is to make disciples, that is, to help people become followers of Christ. How is that done? Well, answering that question is a dilemma the Church has faced throughout the ages. The variety of opinions on the matter is reflected in the variety of Christian denominations. Each Christian denomination has its strengths and its weaknesses. Yet, when it comes to making disciples, there is no formula or denominational program that guarantees people will become followers of Christ. According to Matthew 28, the only way to make disciples is by baptizing them and teaching them. It is our human nature to create shortcuts in order to make things easier. That's exactly what the Church has done with baptism and discipleship. In reality, many denominational rituals and practices are attempted shortcuts to the Great Commission, but there are no shortcuts to discipleship.

To some people, the end of the first gospel may not seem that challenging. All you have to do is make sure someone is baptized and that they go through some form of religious instruction. Undoubtedly, baptism has become one of the most recognized rites in Christianity, but is that what the Great Commission challenges us to do? Was Christ challenging us to engage in a religious ritual? Understanding the ministry of Christ recorded in the gospels and the fact that He so often challenged empty religious rituals, why would Jesus leave His Church with the command to engage in the ritual act of baptism? No doubt, making a public commitment to follow Christ, which is symbolized in the baptismal experience, is important to the Christian community. The Great Commission begs the question; "What is Jesus really challenging us to do?"

What if Christ was using the Greek term *baptizo* "to baptize" to imply the concept of immersion, which is the original nuance of the term, not a ritual? Furthermore, what if Jesus was using the nuance of the Greek word *onoma* "name" to imply nature? It's clear that when Jesus' told his disciples in John 14:13, "whatever you ask in My name, that I will do,"(NKJV) He was encouraging them to pray with His desires, His will, His heart—in essence, to pray in Jesus' "name" is to pray with Jesus' nature. Read with this understanding, the end of Matthew 28 is incredibly challenging because it teaches that the Great Commission is to "make disciples of all the nations, immersing them in the nature of the Father and of the Son and of the Holy Spirit." This is the ultimate mission of the Church—to connect to the Living God through worship and service in such a way that when people are around the Church they are immersed in the nature of God. Thus, the only way you can make a disciple is by being one.

This brings us to a significant spiritual truth. God and Satan actually have the same primary method of operation, that is, both prefer to use people to influence people. That said, consider the societal impact when the influence of Christianity is intentionally suppressed by the government.

I'm always amazed when people are surprised at the results of recent surveys indicating that Christianity's influence is waning and that people are more accepting of non-Christian lifestyles such as heterosexual co-habitation and homosexuality. What else did you expect? The results of the surveys didn't just happen. Rather, the results of the surveys are the intended results of a culture that supports the private practice of Christianity, but does not allow for a public expression of the same. For example, we have educated an entire generation in the public school system in a manner that disparages religion. Should we expect that this generation should become more religious? Our cultural shifts are very much by design, that is, the design of secularists. As was stated in the introduction, we should never again ask the question; "How did our nation get here (e.g. abortion, overwhelming debt, same-sex marriage, rampant divorce, etc.)?" From now on, the question is always, "Where else would you expect to be in a society that exalts the individual, pursues happiness at all costs, and forces the Church into the closet?" The decline of Christianity in the West is the direct result of decades of religious suppression via the courts, but the courts are only one reason Christianity's influence has declined.

When people see that the essence of a worship service involves rituals void of any life-impacting power, then there is no reason we should expect them to remain involved in the church. However, when people see the presence and power of God making a difference in the world around them, then they will stay. Fulfilling the Great Commission makes a difference in the world. Christians are called by God to make a difference in the world. The Church of the 21st century must be courageous enough to reflect a strength that has long been absent in Western Christianity. If the Church is going to fulfill the Great Commission, then it needs to initiate a Reformation in Responsibility by refusing to obey the government when the government asks the Church for a greater allegiance than the allegiance that should be given to God. This point will be discussed further in the next few essays.

Essay 16
Responsible Theology

Mark 12:30-31 – "'You shall love the LORD your God with all your heart, with all your soul, with all your mind, and with all your strength.' This is the first commandment, and the second, like it, is this: 'You shall love your neighbor as yourself.' There is no other commandment greater than these."(NKJV)

Biblical theology teaches that God has given human beings the ability to choose right or wrong, and He will hold them accountable for their choices. God desires that humans cooperate with His work in the world around them. Biblical admonitions such as; "refuse evil and choose good" or "seek the Lord and live" or "choose this day whom you will serve" prove that we have a choice in deciding how we will live our lives. The only question is: "What will we do with the free will that God has given us?" Space and prudence do not permit this work to get into a lengthy discussion of divine predestination and human free will—a topic that has been debated by Christian theologians throughout the ages. Suffice it to say that the debate continues because predestination and free will are both part of biblical theology. In essence, human responsibility and divine sovereignty are not in competition with one another. They complement one other. The fact that God's agenda will be accomplished despite the fact that most humans do not cooperate with God's work in the world is the greatest proof of God's sovereignty. God knows what we will do with our choices, and based on that foreknowledge God determines us to specific ends. That's precisely what Romans 8:29-30 teaches:

> For whom He foreknew, He also predestined to be conformed to the image of His Son, that He might be the firstborn among many brethren. Moreover whom He predestined, these He also called; whom He called, these He also justified; and whom He justified, these He also glorified. (NKJV)

If you work the text backwards, it actually makes more sense. Those who are glorified (attain to the kingdom of heaven) are those who were justified (accepted through the atoning work of Christ and sanctified by their cooperation with the Holy Spirit). Those who were justified are those who were called (led by the Holy Spirit). Those who were called were also predestined (God determines how they fit into the overarching divine plan). Yet, you cannot overlook the last aspect, or first aspect depending on how you're reading the text. God predestined those whom He foreknew. Thus, predestination, from the perspective of Romans 8, is based on God's foreknowledge. One might ask; "Foreknowledge of what?" Answer: God's foreknowledge of how an individual will or will not cooperate with the work of the Holy Spirit in the world.

Belief is only the beginning, not the totality, of the Christian life.

There is a doctrine that has been forgotten in many Christian circles—the Latin translation of which is, "do what is in you." Essentially, the doctrine teaches that salvation is ultimately a work of God, but God is not going to save someone who is not willing to do his/her best to serve Him and have a relationship with Him. The doctrine, like most doctrines, has slightly different perspectives depending on the theologian discussing it. God's grace is apparent and active, in varying degrees, in every person's life. Understanding the call to "do what is in you" is essentially the call to cooperate with the work of God to your fullest capacity. When you do that, God will continue working with you—ultimately saving you. This is consistent with biblical theology from two perspectives; first, it maintains God's sovereignty in the process of salvation. Secondly, it maintains the necessity of human responsibility in the process of salvation—a point that has been underemphasized in modern Christian theology. A valid critique of the "do what is in you" doctrine is the subjectivity of knowing whether or not one has actually done what is in him/her. Once again, such a concern is focused primarily on individual salvation and happiness not divine sovereignty or human responsibility.

A theology of responsibility challenges a person to a lifelong process of doing what is in him/her, that is, doing his/her best for God. Indeed, as many authors have pointed out, salvation is a process; a process that involves being justified, sanctified, and glorified by faith. Everything begins and ends with faith in God. John 8:31-32 says, "Then Jesus said to those Jews who believed Him, 'If you abide in My word, you are My disciples indeed, and you shall know the truth, and the truth shall make you free.'"(NKJV) Notice the audience, "those… who believed." Belief is only the beginning, not the totality, of the Christian life. After a person has made the decision to believe, then the next step is to abide in Christ's word, that is, to follow Christ's teaching. This is also an act of faith. When a person believes by faith that God's commands are important, then he/she will strive to "do his/her best" to obey the commands of God. Then, after a period of time striving to follow God's commands, the person becomes a disciple. Belief doesn't make a disciple. Abiding in God's Word makes a disciple, but the Christian life doesn't end there. The disciple of Christ is always growing in his/her understanding of the truth. Many people understand the commands of God theoretically, but only a disciple of Christ understands, via experience, the truth of God. It's one thing to have someone tell you about a relationship with God. It's another matter altogether to have a relationship with God and experience God's truth. After you have become a disciple, then you begin to know the truth—then you are set free. Thus, there is a five step process in responsible Christian theology: 1) a person believes in Christ; 2) a person abides in the Word of God; 3) a person becomes a disciple; 4) a person knows God's truth through experience; and finally 5) a person is set free in Christ. Apart from a miraculous work of God, a person doesn't get from step one to step five without going through the difficult and lengthy process of steps two, three, and four. A Reformation in Responsibility requires responsible theology. The Church of the 21st century needs to have the integrity to tell people that the challenges and responsibilities of the Christian life are significant. Furthermore, the Church must have the courage to follow Christ's example and allow people to walk away and fail if they are not willing to accept the demands of discipleship (Mark 10:17-23).

Questions for Reflection:
What is your initial reaction to this essay?

What did you agree/disagree with in this essay? Why?

What is your reaction to the story in Mark 10:17-23?

In Mark 10:21, what did Jesus do that demonstrated love for the one who was seeking eternal life?

My summary of this essay:

Essay 17
A New Ethic for a New Era

Philippians 2:4 – Let each of you look out not only for his own interests, but also for the interests of others. (NKJV)

On January 22, 1993, I stood on the graduation field with U.S. Army Ranger Class 2-93. Due to the cold winter, only a small group of us made it straight through the course without recycling one of the phases. The instructors referred to us as, "the frozen chosen." Ranger School is, in the words of Dickens, "the best of times and the worst of times." Few things are more rewarding than being on the graduation field with your fellow Rangers, and even fewer things are as hard as the character lessons learned during the course. If Ranger School teaches anything, it teaches the importance of taking responsibility for your actions. The Ranger Creed, formed from the word "R-A-N-G-E-R," includes the following vow: "Never will I fail my comrades… I will shoulder more than my share of the task whatever it may be, one-hundred-percent and then some." The worst insult an instructor could give a Ranger candidate would be to call him a "spotlight ranger." The term is used to describe a soldier that only performs when he is being watched by the instructors; in other words, a spotlight ranger is in it for himself not for the rest of the unit. Spotlight rangers don't last long in elite military units because everyone knows that a unit won't last long with spotlight rangers. The strength behind elite Special Operations Forces (SOF) is the ethic that guides their members. They have an incredible sense of commitment and responsibility to one another, and in turn they have a common commitment to something that is bigger than the unit itself. Their priority of concern is the mission, the unit, and then the individual. If our nation wants to show respect for the sacrifice of its Special Operations Forces then it should follow their example by encouraging people to live for something bigger than the pursuit of individual happiness. President Kennedy, a strong supporter of SOF, will long be remembered for saying, "Ask not what your country can do for you; ask what you can do for your country." Indeed, members of SOF are the embodiment of that ideal.

As a nation however, we have ignored that ideal and we promote the opposite attitude, "Ask not what you can do for your country; ask what your country can do for you." The same attitude is reflected in American industry via the unions, "Ask not what you can do for your company; ask what your company can do for you." It should be no surprise that our theology is the same, "Ask not what you can do for God; ask what God can do for you." This is a highly problematic attitude. The dominant ethic of our society teaches us that the individual doesn't exist to contribute to the good of the larger society. Rather, the larger society exists to serve the good of the individual—even the most criminal and dysfunctional individuals among us. How does a nation succeed with this attitude? Americans no longer work for the good of their companies. Americans expect companies to work for their good. How does a nation's industry survive with such an attitude? Answer—it doesn't survive in America, it goes overseas. Theologically, Christ said a proper prayer begins by acknowledging God's transcendence, "Our Father who is in Heaven,

Part of a Reformation in Responsibility is teaching people that there are things that are more important than the individual's pursuit of happiness.

Holy is your name," and asking for God's perfect will to be accomplished, "Your kingdom come. Your will be done," but that's not our prayer. Our prayer is, "My kingdom come, my will be done." Part of a Reformation in Responsibility is teaching people that there are things that are more important than the individual's pursuit of happiness. Serving the larger community is always more rewarding than serving oneself, and nothing is more rewarding than serving God.

For a responsible society, service for the good of the whole is not regulated by the government. It's managed by the people. The more responsible a society is and the more communities work together, the less need there is for government regulation. Government over-involvement is an ominous sign of rampant irresponsibility which, in the long run, leads to social insecurity. Thus, the only way to reverse our nation's downward spiral is for the government to start letting our people take responsibility for their own decisions and actions. Not only is this important because it is in the best interest of our people, it's also important because we are in a very dangerous situation as a nation. Our government plays the part of the protector of the people when at the same time it is responsible for making the most destructive decisions our nation has witnessed in decades. Our government struggles to create new jobs, but it is responsible for legislating labor laws that forced American industry overseas. Our government wants to sue big banks for irresponsible loans, but it was responsible for opening the door to irresponsible lending by pressuring the banks to put lower income families into homes they could not afford and to provide foolish options like interest only loans. The danger with all of this is that we have become conditioned to depend on the government at a time when the government is making incredibly irresponsible decisions.

It's understandable that a people would be inclined to depend on a responsible government that makes good decisions, and that was our case in the past. However, allowing ourselves to become dependent on an irresponsible government that has marginalized its civil religion, destroyed its national industry, and drained its national economy is the height of irresponsibility. Sadly, it's clear that the government has not finished its destructive course as it is currently in the process of destroying the public education system and dismantling traditional marriage as the foundation of our society. If the people of the United States allow the government to control public education and topple traditional marriage, then we will find that our current struggles are nothing compared to the struggles we will face in the future. In order to succeed, America must reorder its responsibilities.

A Reformation in Responsibility must usher in a new ethic— an ethic of responsibility.

A Reformation in Responsibility must usher in a new ethic—an ethic of responsibility. People are primarily responsible to three things in life: 1) people are responsible to God; 2) people are responsible to others (beginning with their family); 3) people are responsible for pursuing their desires and happiness. The order is important because fulfilling our responsibilities to God, family, and society, enables us to pursue happiness in the proper manner. If a person reverses the order and pursues happiness while showing little regard for God, family, and society, then failure and frustration are inevitable. Thus, our society is frustrated and failing because we have our priorities and responsibilities backwards. In our maddening pursuit of happiness, we have abandoned our responsibilities to our families and society. It is time for the Church to lead society once again by teaching a theology and ethic of responsibility—a threefold ethic of responsibility. Like the use of the word "Ranger" in forming the Ranger Creed, one can use the word "God" as a tool for properly understanding the priority of one's responsibilities.

Fulfill your responsibilities to ....**God**.
Fulfill your responsibilities to ....**O**thers
Fulfill your ....**D**esires.

Questions for Reflection:
What is your initial reaction to this essay?

What did you agree/disagree with in this essay? Why?

Are your priorities in the right place? Why or why not? If not, what can you do to set your priorities right?

My summary of this essay:

Essay 18
Majority Rights & Privatized Religion

Proverbs 14:28b… a prince without subjects has nothing.(NLT)

We have already made the point that majority opinions are just as important, and in some cases are more important, than individual and minority opinions. This is true because, in the case of any nation, the entire social foundation can be destabilized when the sentiments of the majority are pushed aside in order to accommodate the sentiments of the minority. The more a government ignores the majority of citizens in favor of a minority of citizens, the faster that government will decline precisely because it is out of touch with the majority of its people. A disregard for majority rights has been commonplace in America for a number of decades. The reason the majority has not resisted is because, up to this point, the majority has been convinced that democracy and constitutionality demand that their sentiments take a back seat to individual/minority sentiments. Yet, this was never meant to be. If the subjugation of the majority was intended by the founders of our nation, then they would have done the things that we are doing now, but they didn't. The fact that our founders did not force religion out of the public square is proof that a complete separation between religion and politics was not their intent. The fact that our founders did not endorse same-sex marriage is proof that constitutionality and human rights does not require such an endorsement now. The fact that our founders were willing to stand up and fight for their right to govern themselves is proof that the issue is worth standing up and fighting for now.

We the people have abdicated our right to govern ourselves, and we have given that right to the secular courts. For years, secularists have been telling us that the constitution is a living, breathing document. That is true. As one generation interprets the Constitution, or better said, interprets interpretations of the Constitution, the next generation will likely see things differently and so on until the majority of people realize that many modern constitutional interpretations no longer represent the essential principles of the Constitution. This is precisely what happened with the Western Church leading up to the 16th century. The Catholic Church was so reliant on layers of biblical interpretation that it became clear that, in some ways, the Church was no longer true to the essential teachings of the Bible and Christianity. The same holds true for secular politicians and judges in 21st century America. Judges, lawyers, and politicians have been relying on layers of constitutional interpretation rather than relying on the essential teachings of the Constitution itself. This was a nation of the people by the people for the people, but that is no longer the case. Secularist politicians have become so brazen that some of them openly declare to the world that we are not a Christian nation, despite the fact that over 70% of Americans still consider themselves Christian. Why would American leaders say such a thing? First, according to secularism, religion has no place in politics. Of course, science, which has become the religion of the secularist, can drive entire policies and public school curriculums, but they believe religion should remain in the closet. Second, and more concerning, our leaders are less concerned with the majority and more concerned about appeasing the minority. Another classic example of irresponsible individualism and minority rights—overlook 70% and coddle to 2%!

If the majority of the citizens of this country are professing Christians, then their right to practice their religion in public must be returned to them. We have long functioned under the idea that religion is a private matter, but nothing is private. I remember the Commandant of Cadets during my years at The Citadel saying to me on more than one occasion, "Responsibility is doing your duty when no one is watching." What we are in private always has public ramifications. Here's something to consider. If one's private life and public life are so easily separated, then what is the homosexual agenda all about? For years homosexuals argued that what they do in private shouldn't affect how they are accepted in public. Naively, people accepted that argument as if it actually made sense. Now, we know the truth. What one generation desires to do in private, the next generation will desire to do in public. Fair enough. If homosexuals are encouraged to be public about their beliefs and practices, why shouldn't Christians receive the same encouragement? You see, the courts have convinced us that religion is a private matter (see essay 6) but that is a great injustice and a violation of the rights of the majority of the population.

Local communities should be able to express their religion and educate their children without the government telling them how to do it. That is the principle upon which America was founded.

In order for things to change, religion should be privatized not private. When something is "privatized," it is addressed and regulated by the majority of the people. Thus, decisions on how to appropriate religion into society should be made by local communities not the federal government. For example, if a public school system in the Bible Belt desires to have a prayer at the beginning of the school day because 95% of the teachers, faculty, administrators, and students share the same beliefs, then the government does not have the right to tell them that they can't pray—especially when their tax money is paying for the school. Local communities should be able to express their religion and educate their children without the government telling them how to do it. That is the principle upon which America was founded. So then, what is an individual with a minority opinion to do if the majority of people around him/her are living out their beliefs? Well, there are a couple of options for the individual or minority group: 1) understand that it is the right of the majority to live out their beliefs and graciously deal with it; or 2) move to a place where you won't have to deal with it. Of course, this flies in the face of the decisions that Western courts have been forcing for decades. In the name of individual rights and the separation of religion and state, the courts force the majority of Americans to stop doing what they desire to do and they allow the minority to determine the way the majority will live. Americans should do everything they can to stop such judicial tyranny.

Allowing people to decide the degree to which religion will play a role in their community will provide another benefit to our society. It will provide a perfect case study for how to govern and educate a community (morally, financially, and politically). There is no doubt that those who hold to traditional values and common sense will outperform those who wholeheartedly embrace secularism. The proof is in the politics. Through its irresponsible individualism and welfare philosophies, secularism has taken the most powerful nation on earth and brought it to the point of moral and financial bankruptcy in 66 years (America from 1946-2012).

Christianity is the civil religion of America, but religious Americans need to start standing up for their beliefs. It's time for the people of the United States to restore the essence of our liberty—a government of the people by the people for the people. America was never meant to be a government of the courts by the secularists for the minority. A Reformation in Responsibility involves a resurrection of majority rights and the privatizing of religion.

Questions for Reflection:
What is your initial reaction to this essay?

What did you agree/disagree with in this essay? Why?

How do you think the privatization of religion would play itself out in the United States with respect to public schools?

My summary of this essay:

Essay 19

Civil Disobedience: the Church as a Fourth Check and Balance

Daniel 3:18 – We want to make it clear to you, Your Majesty, that we will never serve your gods or worship the gold statue you have set up.(NLT)

At this point many people, especially those involved in law, will begin to think about various court cases and the precedents that have been set by those cases for the contemporary understanding of the separation of Church and State. Yet, that is part of the problem. Our system of constitutional interpretation is broken. Appealing to the courts to fix the irresponsible individualism of our era would be like Martin Luther appealing to the Catholic Church to begin the Reformation. Interestingly, Luther did appeal to the Catholic Church, and we know the outcome. Likewise, appealing to our broken judicial system will only lead to more frustration. It is time for a change. It is time to move away from the irresponsible individualism that is promoted by our judicial system. It is time for Christians to recognize that their role is to stand against the system—not to become part of the system. It is time for the Church to start saying to the government, "No." When the government, via the courts, tells the majority of people that they cannot pray in the name of their God at tax sponsored events, that is a direct violation of religious freedom. If it were not for tax payers there would be no such thing as tax sponsored events. Thus, if the majority of taxpayers desire to pray at a tax sponsored event, then that is their constitutional right. If the government tells them otherwise, then they have the right to stand against the government. Interestingly, our founding fathers knew that this time would come.

As indicated in Essay 4, the second sentence of our Declaration of Independence is by far the most famous sentence in the entire declaration, but what comes after that sentence is more relevant for our current national crisis. Let's look at a portion of the Declaration again with italics added for emphasis:

> We hold these truths to be self-evident, that all men are created equal, that they are endowed by their Creator with certain unalienable rights, that among these are life, liberty and the pursuit of happiness. That to secure these rights, *governments are instituted among men, deriving their just powers from the consent of the governed.* That *whenever any form of government becomes destructive to these ends, it is the right of the people to alter or to abolish it,* and to institute new government, laying its foundation on such principles and organizing its powers in such form, as to them shall seem most likely to effect their safety and happiness. Prudence, indeed, will dictate that *governments long established should not be changed for light and transient causes*; and accordingly all *experience hath shown that mankind are more disposed to suffer, while evils are sufferable, than to right themselves by abolishing the forms to which they are accustomed.*

That is exactly what we need to hear today. Prudence instructs us not to challenge the government over "light and transient" matters, but experience teaches us that most societies are "disposed to suffer" rather than "abolish the forms [of government] to which they are accustomed." For the last sixty years, we have been accustomed to a government that has—under the guise of individual rights and constitutionality—disparaged the majority of our citizens, trivialized our civil religion, driven our industry overseas, drained our finances through entitlement programs, and is attempting to restructure marriage according to the passing pleasures of sin. There is but one question to present to our nation: "Are these 'light and transient' matters, or are these matters of national and social security?" Most rational people would certainly argue for the latter. The time has come for the majority to stand up.

Recently, I had a conversation with a stranger while waiting for our vehicles at a car wash. The Arab Spring came up in our conversation, and I said, "It's amazing to think that a government is really nothing more than volunteerism." To that he replied, "People just don't understand how hard our volunteers work and how much we should appreciate them." He didn't get what I was saying and I didn't bother trying to explain myself. Our Declaration of Independence says that governments derive "their just powers from the consent of the governed." In other words, all governmental systems are very fragile. Every form of government is dependent on the willingness of its subjects to obey, that is, to voluntarily support the government. Now, some would argue that people have no choice but to support oppressive regimes. That is not true. It doesn't matter if you are dealing with an oppressive dictatorship, a communist regime, a democracy, or a democratic republic, no form of government can take away a

> *American Christians have demonstrated that their allegiance is more to social security and Statehood than it is to the Living God and the teachings of Christianity.*

person's freedom of choice. People's choices may cost them their lives, but they still have the freedom to choose (Daniel 3:1-30). That is the power of responsible individualism. You see, when the time comes that a government disrespects and/or disagrees with the majority of its people, it will not take many decades before the volunteerism that is reflected in obedience to the government is replaced with civil disobedience, reformation, or revolution, as in the case of America's early history. Secularists have forgotten this truth and many other important truths from our past (e.g. the importance of traditional marriage, the absurdity of overwhelming debt, the stabilizing effect of faith, etc.).

When the government demands a greater allegiance than the allegiance we owe to God, a Reformation in Responsibility demands that the Church engage in civil disobedience.

What is surprising is that our current government thinks it can undermine our people's sense of responsibility to God, parents, educational leaders, and even law enforcement, but somehow the government expects the people to maintain a sense of responsibility and respect toward the State—especially towards the courts. However, that's impossible. A government cannot undermine divine authority, parental authority, and local police authority without undermining its own judicial authority in the process. We are already seeing the cracks in the dam of judicial authority. People are starting to realize that the courts are overstepping their bounds (e.g. telling communities when and how to pray, the reversal of Proposition 8 in CA, forcing people to buy into a government health care system). If the courts continue to ignore the voice of the people, the people will eventually ignore the voice of the courts. Such a move will not be rooted in anarchy but rather, it will be rooted in responsibility. When irresponsible leaders push their people to the limits, the people will take responsibility for the direction of the nation.

To date, American Christians have demonstrated that their allegiance is more to social security and Statehood than it is to the Living God and the teachings of Christianity. In America, Christians will toe the line and do exactly what the State tells them to do. If the public school system tells teachers they can't share their religion because it's an abuse of the power that comes with their position, then the vast majority of teachers will salute the administration and refuse to share their faith. Hypocritically, if influential leaders in the Department of Education want to promote homosexuality and transgender activity, we are to believe that's not an abuse of the power that comes with their positions. For the Church to be a significant part of a Reformation in Responsibility, the Church must encourage its members to stand up for their rights. It is time for the Church to take the lead in challenging our current system of constitutional interpretation.

In short, the American Church should have the courage to change its own culture before it goes on the mission field to help change the cultures of other nations. In order to minister to our individualistic and irresponsible culture, the 21st century Church must look to the example of the Early Church. The early Church grew because its leaders and followers actually believed in the message they proclaimed. In Acts 5, after some of the apostles were thrown into prison for proclaiming the Gospel of Christ, the authorities threatened the apostles with the admonition not to teach again in Jesus' name. Their response in Acts 5:29 is an example for every generation, "We ought to obey God rather than men." That was the unwavering assertion of the 1st century

Church. The Church in the 21st century would do well to follow that example. When the government demands a greater allegiance than the allegiance we owe to God, a Reformation in Responsibility demands that the Church engage in civil disobedience.

Questions for Reflection:
What is your initial reaction to this essay?

What did you agree/disagree with in this essay? Why?

If the LGBT community is willing to engage in civil disobedience in order to promote their agenda, why shouldn't the Church be willing to engage in civil disobedience to promote the Kingdom of God? Who do you think is more committed to their cause, the LGBT community or the Christian community?

My summary of this essay:

Essay 20
The Reformation

Without a Reformation in Responsibility, the United States will not prosper in the future. Over the last hundred years, we can point to specific changes that have contributed to our national decline. Thus, the following areas that have experienced change are also the areas that need to be reformed: 1) the waning influence of Christianity requires us to reform the Church; 2) the promotion of irresponsible individualism requires us to reform our civil philosophy; 3) judicial tyranny demands that we reform the role of the courts; 4) the failure of public education necessitates a reform of public education; 5) the significant reduction in American industry requires us to reform American industry; 6) the increase in entitlement programs makes it essential that we reform entitlement programs and; 7) a general lack of servant leadership at the highest levels of American politics should prompt us to reform politics. If the United States is to succeed in the future, we must reform each of these areas.

Our final conversation will provide some bullet statements that are essential for reform. Determining exactly how these reforms are to take place is well beyond the scope of our conversation. That is the goal of elected officials. Thus, the people of the United States must elect the right officials in order to bring about the right kind of change. If we do not elect the right officials, then our problems will be perpetuated by leaders who cannot jettison the irresponsible individualism that has shaped the theology, philosophy, and policy making of our nation. If a Reformation in Responsibility is to occur, then our theology, philosophy, and policy making must be rooted in a responsible worldview. Furthermore, as has already been stated, this Reformation must start with the Church. With that said, the following are some guiding principles that people can rally around in order to initiate a Reformation in Responsibility:

Reforming the Church:
1) A civil religion is the religion most reflected in the history and/or values of a people. Thus, Christianity is the civil religion of the people of the United States.
2) The individual is not the focal point of Christian theology. God is the focal point of Christian theology.
3) The 21st century Church must be more committed to biblical theology and traditional Christian morality than to denominational polity and practice.
4) The government does not have the right to tell the majority of taxpayers that they cannot pray in the name of their God at taxpayer sponsored institutions or events (i.e. any government institution or event).
5) When the government violates the free exercise of religion, the Church should courageously stand against the government.
6) The Church should take the lead in helping the poor. However, the Church has no moral obligation to help those who are deliberately lazy and irresponsible. Responsible theology promotes responsible living. Those who will not work will not eat (2 Thessalonians 3:10).
7) The government should not be responsible for taking care of the sick and dying. Families and churches are responsible for taking care of the sick and dying. Furthermore, the Church should be a strong promoter of environmental stewardship.
8) Holding people accountable for their actions is the great-

est sign of respect. Thus, the concept of hell is a concept that actually respects the potential of human beings. Where there is no accountability, there is no respect.
9) Pastors and church leaders who embrace heterodoxy and reject orthodoxy should have the courage to acknowledge that they are agnostics not Christians.
10) Congregations that entertain politically correct agnostics in the pulpit do not deserve the allegiance of committed Christians.
11) If the Church would proclaim a responsible theology, then our society might embrace a responsible philosophy.

Reforming Our Civil Philosophy:
12) We are not the most complete society to ever exist. There are past societies that were, in many ways, better than our society.
13) We have made significant technological advances, but we are not the smartest society to exist.
14) The irresponsible pursuit of happiness needs to be balanced with individual responsibility.
15) A self-centered pursuit of happiness will never make a person happy.
16) People will find happiness when they fulfill their responsibilities to God and society (beginning with their families).
17) Leaders who believe an individual's pursuit of happiness is the primary goal of society are a major part of our problem.
18) The society does not exist to serve the needs and desires of the individual.
19) The individual is best served when he/she serves toward

the good of the larger society.
20) Our society should not assume responsibility for those who are blatantly irresponsible.
21) We are failing to succeed because we will not let individuals fail in order to let the nation succeed.
22) Leaders who refuse to let people fail are a major part of our crisis of responsibility.

Reforming the Courts:
23) A majority group and a minority group are essentially the same thing, that is, both are made up of individuals.
24) It makes little sense for the courts to worry about appeasing small groups of individuals while at the same time disregarding the sentiments of much larger groups of individuals.
25) Irresponsible Individualism subjugates the sentiments of the majority to the desires of the minority.
26) Responsible individualism acknowledges that majority rights/opinions are just as important as minority rights/opinions.
27) The courts do not exist to protect the individual's pursuit of happiness however he/she might define, "happiness." The courts exist to protect the individual's right to live responsibly in a responsible society.
28) It is unethical and unconstitutional for the courts to force the majority to accept values and lifestyles that they do not agree with (e.g. same-sex marriage and polygamy).
29) Judges that ignore the voice of the majority can only expect that the time will come when the majority will ignore the voice of the courts.
30) Judges hold people accountable for their decisions. Thus, judges should be held accountable for their decisions

(e.g. If a judge lets a murder, with repeat offenses, out on probation and the murder kills again, then the judge should be held accountable for that murder).
31) Judges should seek to limit the amount of litigation taking place in our society in order to force people to take responsibility for their problems and solutions.
32) The more laws a people need, the more lawless the people. Laws, litigation, and lawlessness increase and decrease proportionately.
33) Judges who refuse to acknowledge the importance of majority rights are a major part of our problem and should be replaced.

Reforming Education:
34) Education is not a right. Education is a privilege.
35) Ultimately, administrators and teachers are not responsible for student success. Students and families are responsible for student success.
36) Some students and families, who reflect blatant irresponsibility in secondary education, should be left behind.
37) The Federal Department of Education should be reduced significantly so that it only reports on the best educational practices and procedures, and leaves implementation to the local level.
38) The Federal Department of Education, which is funded by taxpayers, does not have the right to indoctrinate the children of the United States when said indoctrination goes against the beliefs and values of the majority of taxpayers.
39) The Department of Education is failing to succeed because it refuses to allow people to fail in order to succeed.

40) Reason and science are extremely important, but they are not more important than the arts and humanities. Reason and science have not served us well in all circumstances.
41) The separation of faith and reason is a modern myth. There are not enough facts to live by facts alone. Thus, all people live by faith. Faith and reason are commensurate with one another and local communities should be able to decide how they will incorporate faith into their educational programs.
42) Localizing education forces communities and families to become responsible for their children. The degree to which communities and families are responsible for education is the degree to which education will be successful.
43) Politicians who understand the advantages and strengths that result from localized education should encourage their school systems to become independent of government funding.
44) Politicians who believe the federal government should be responsible for educating our children should be replaced.

Reforming American Industry:
45) Industrial success is imperative for the success of any nation.
46) Labor laws will always be important, but labor laws need to be balanced with the need for American industry.
47) Greed is the impetus for many of our nation's labor laws.
48) Excessive labor laws result in a threefold loss: the loss of the American industry, the loss of American labor, and

the loss of high quality American products.
49) Corporations that do not treat their employees right will eventually succumb to their injustices.
50) If a corporation does not care about its people, then it will not care about its product because it only cares about its profit.
51) The government needs to encourage localized commerce.
52) Corporate leaders need to have more allegiance to our society than to making money.
53) Leaders who understand our crisis will do everything possible to rebuild American industry.
54) Politicians who are unfriendly to American industry need to be replaced.
55) Communities will grow when people support one another.

Reforming Entitlement Programs:
56) Entitlement programs should promote responsibility among our people.
57) We need to eliminate irresponsible entitlement programs and allow irresponsible people to fail.
58) The government should not be responsible for taking care of the senior adult population under the guise of social security. That is the responsibility of families and Churches.
59) Social security will never be found in a government check.
60) Government Social Security fosters irresponsibility.
61) Government Social Security is unsustainable.
62) Government Social Security should be responsibly and incrementally eliminated.

63) True social security only comes from two sources, God and the people in your life.
64) Politicians who think the "rich," which is a rather ambiguous term, should pay more in order to support government entitlement programs are irresponsible welfare politicians.
65) Welfare politicians will lead any nation to bankruptcy (e.g. Greece, Spain, Italy, the United States, etc.).
66) Irresponsible people will always vote for welfare politicians. Responsible people will always oppose welfare politicians.

Reforming Politics:
67) If a person has consistently demonstrated that he/she will not live responsibly via property ownership and paying taxes, then he/she should not be able to vote. If a person cannot manage his/her own home responsibly, why should he/she vote on managing the country?
68) Two choices is not much of a choice for a nation that prides itself on the ability to choose. Thus, a two party system should be challenged by the acceptance of new political parties.
69) Politicians who vigorously promote equal opportunity still don't understand our crisis of responsibility. When a nation forces its institutions and businesses to hire under qualified people, it is a guarantee for long term failure—not just the failure of individual businesses and institutions but the failure of the nation at large.
70) Politicians should set an example for a Reformation in Responsibility by doing away with their entitlement plans. Politicians should demonstrate that people should not rely on the government for their retirement.

71) Politicians that reject traditional values should be replaced by politicians that value the wisdom of the past.
72) Politicians that promote government responsibility should be replaced with politicians that promote individual responsibility.
73) Politicians that promote the minority opinion over and against the majority opinion should be replaced with politicians that understand the importance of majority rights.
74) Politicians that promote federalized education should be replaced with politicians that promote localized education.
75) Politicians that support activist judges should be replaced with politicians that support a true democratic process.
76) Politicians that are not friendly to American industry should be replaced with politicians that understand the importance of American industry.
77) Politicians that cannot balance the national budget should be replaced with politicians that can balance the budget and create a budget surplus.

Nations are governed by laws. Laws are governed by people. People are governed by philosophy and theology. If you change the civil philosophy and theology, then you will change the people. If you change the people, then you will change the laws. If you change the laws, then you will change the nation. Are you willing to break free from the irresponsible theology and philosophy that has marred our culture? Are you willing to become part of a Reformation in Responsibility? If so, then you must determine how to put these concepts into action, and take responsibility for your part in the Reformation.

About the author:

Rit Varriale is originally from Schenectady, New York. His early religious influence was in the Roman Catholic, Dutch Reformed, and Calvary Chapel traditions. He became involved in the Baptist tradition while attending The Citadel, the Military College of South Carolina. During his senior year at The Citadel, he served as the Regimental Commander for the Corps of Cadets. Upon graduation from The Citadel in 1992, Rit was commissioned as an officer in the United States Army and was assigned to the 82nd Airborne Division from 1992-1996 serving as a platoon leader and company executive officer with A Troop 1/17 Cavalry. During that time, he received the Outstanding Leadership award for U.S. Army Ranger Class 2-93, the Senior Parachutist Badge, and the Pathfinder Badge. In 1996, Rit entered the ministry and began his theological training receiving a M.Div. (Campbell University Divinity School) a Th.M. (Duke University Divinity School) and a D.Min. (Princeton Theological Seminary). From 1996-present he has served three congregations in North Carolina. Currently, Rit resides in Shelby, NC with his wife Shannon.